G000122638

COMPILED BY
AUBREY MALONE

SBH Scotland Books

Published in 2017 by SBH Scotland Books

ISBN Paperback: 978-1-9999250-0-0
Ebook: 978-1-9999250-1-7

A CIP catalogue copy of this book can be
found in the British Library.

Disclaimer: Every effort has been made to attribute
the quotations in this collection to the correct source.
Should there be any omissions or errors in this respect we
apologise, and shall be pleased to make the appropriate
acknowledgements in any future editions.

Published with the help of Indie Authors World

IndieAuthors
World

INTRODUCTION

Spina Bifida Hydrocephalus Scotland support over 3500 babies, children, young people, adults and their carers affected by the complex disabilities of spina bifida and/or hydrocephalus. They are one of Scotland's oldest self-funded charities and this, combined with the fact that my wife, who works as a teacher's aid, had a young girl in her class last year affected by Spina Bifida, meant that I was greatly drawn to the charity as an outlet for this anthology of Scottish quotations. My wife spoke in great length about the courage and determination of the young girl she was supporting, and how laughter seemed to prove a tonic for this pupil, as it is for so many of us struggling with health problems or challenging circumstances. Freud, of course, pointed out a century ago that humour offers us a healthy means of coping with life stress and this has been backed up by many. 'Against the assault of laughter nothing can stand.' (Mark Twain) 'Always laugh when you can. It is cheap medicine.' (Lord Byron).

Hopefully any readers of this book who are facing daily trials, whatever they may be, will find it possible to gain a little solace from the wit, wisdom and waffle contained in its pages.

The quotes are intended as a rough guide to the eccentric spirit of Scotland with all its figaries and quirks. Perhaps some sail close to the wind of good taste but where would humour be without sarcasm or a salty tongue? I hope no Scot will be offended by the occasional wickedness expressed in

3

them. Of course being Scottish, they'll be quick to rise to their own defence and give an equally wicked barb back!

It always seems worse to see children and young people facing difficulty and this is why one appreciates organisations like Spina Bifida Hydrocephalus Scotland so much. It started life as the Scottish Spina Bifida Association way back in 1965 when a small group of parents whose children had the disabilities banded together to try and raise awareness. Since then it's gone from strength to strength to become the wide-ranging organisation it is today. Receiving little or no statutory funding, it needs £1 million a year to continue its work. Despite their reputation as being tight, the people of Scotland are among the most warmest and generous and their deep- rooted family values and philanthropic approach run deep and the public have generously supported this charity for over 50 years.

All profits from sales will go to the charity so by purchasing this book you are doing your bit to ensure that the charity can continue assisting everyone that approaches them for help for many years to come.

www.sbhscotland.org.uk.

We're fundraising in aid of

Spina Bifida Hydrocephalus Scotland

ABOUT THE AUTHOR

Aubrey Malone was born in the West of Ireland but has spent most of his life in Dublin. He was a primary teacher from 1977-89. After leaving teaching he became a freelance journalist, working for various newspapers and magazines. In 1996 he started writing books. He has written biographies of Ernest Hemingway, Brendan Behan, Tom Jones, Elvis Presley, Tony Curtis and Maureen O'Hara, among others. He has also edited many books of humorous quotations like this one, and has written other books for charitable causes, like 'On the Edge', a study of psychological problems of famous people, 'A Ripe Old Age', a book about the elderly written in conjunction with the Alzheimer Society of Ireland and 'Killing Pain', a biography of Malachy Smyth, who pioneered research into back pain.

ABUSE

I wouldn't sell them a virus. (**Alex Ferguson on rumours he was considering selling Christiano Ronaldo to Real Madrid in 2008**)

When Mariah Carey wanted to get rid of her chewing gum as I was interviewing her, somebody put their hand out to take it. It appeared to be their only job. (**Lorraine Kelly**)

I'm not saying the Scottish Health Service is bad, but one or two hospitals still send their patients to Glasgow Airport for X-rays. (**Allan Morrison**)

I believe you would have condoned the South Sea bubble and the persecution of the Albigenses if they had been carried out in effective colour schemes. (**Saki**)

He can't run, can't tackle and can't head a ball. The only time he goes forward is to toss the coin. (**Tommy Docherty on Ray Wilkins**)

To fail and die young is the only hope for a Scotsman who wishes to remain an artist. (**Oscar Wilde**)

There's a place for the press – but they haven't dug it yet. (**Tommy Docherty**)

Arthur Balfour's impact on history is no more than the whiff of scent on a lady's purse. (**David Lloyd George**)

Thou eunuch of language, thou pimp of gender, thou pickle-herring in the puppet shoe of nonsense. (**Robert Burns to a critic**)

How many Glasgow men does it take to change a toilet roll? Who knows – it never happened. (**Allan Morrison**)

If Tommy Docherty says 'Good morning' to you, check the weather. (**George Best**)

Lady Desborough tells enough white lies to ice a wedding cake. (**Margot Asquith**)

On some flashes of dialogue he talked as if he had a mouthful of lettuce leaves. (**John Parker on Sean Connery in *The Anderson Tapes***)

Gordon Strachan's tongue can kill a man at ten paces. (**Mick Henigan**)

Kenny Dalglish suffers from constipation of the emotions. (**Michael Parkinson**)

If you dropped the FIFA crowd into the ocean, they wouldn't be able to decide if it was wet or not. (**Jake Duncan**)

It makes *Mutiny on the Bounty* look like a United Free Church of Scotland choir outing on a hot June afternoon. (**James T. Cameron on the melodrama of Alastair MacLean's first novel, *HMS Ulysses***)

What is Conrad but the wreck of Robert Louis Stevenson floating about on the slip-slop of Henry James? (**George Moore on Joseph Conrad**)

Ah'm not saying ah don't like the guy but if he snuffed it, ah'd take a kerry-out tae his funeral. (**Michael Munro**)

At a Celtic-Motherwell match, a Celtic supporter, incensed at the referee awarding a penalty against his team, shouted, 'I wish your mother had been on the pill?' (**James A. Simpson**)

A little boy sucking his misogynist thumb and blubbering and carping in the corner of the front bench below the gangway. (**Nicholas Fairbairn on Edward Heath**)

He calls her melancholy. That's because she's got a head like a melon and a face like a collie. (**Stanley Baxter**)

They say true poverty smells filthy sweet. In that case, my father was not truly poor. He smelled of stale tobacco, damp cloth and bad temper. (**Ian Pattison**)

When they put teeth in your mouth, they spoiled a perfectly good bum. (**Billy Connolly**)

I'm looking for Commander James Bond, not an overgrown stunt man. (**Ian Fleming on Sean Connery as 007**)

ACCENTS

You've done awfully well for a man with a speech defect. (**Billy Connolly to Sean Connery at the BAFTA ceremonies in 1999**)

For the benefit of Anglo-Saxon viewers, I wonder if the TV sports presenters would consider using subtitles when interviewing Kenny Dalglish. (**Letter to *The Standard***)

People with phoney accents can't last when they're talking to me. Mine sort of draws their old one out. You can see them fighting it. The Adam's apple falls to the side. (**Billy Connolly**)

The interpreter couldn't understand me. (**Jimmy Nicholl explaining why a meeting with two Russian football players that was supposed to take 5 minutes lasted 45 minutes in 1996**)

Scottish accents have deteriorated so much, even Parliament debate now sounds like the rowdier exchanges on the Ibrox terracing. (**George MacDonald Fraser**)

Sean Connery gets a call from his agent one day. 'I've got a job for you,' he says. 'It starts tomorrow early. You'll have to be there by 10-ish.' 'Tennish?' Connery replies, 'but I don't even have a racquet.' (**Internet joke**)

She didn't wink, but her voice did. (**George MacDonald Fraser**)

ACTORS AND ACTING

My main motivation as an actor? Fear of being crap. (**Ewan McGregor**).

I played a nasty, manipulative guy in *Trainspotting*. A lot of people will say 'Typecasting'. (**Irvine Welsh**)

When people warned me there would be long periods out of work if I became an actor I couldn't keep a straight face. Because that's exactly what I had in mind. (**Bill Nighy**)

Film stars have a nervousness which goes right to the edge. You have to use this to get the best out of these deep-sea monsters. (**Alexander Mackendrick**)

You're always comforted by other actors when you're involved in something awful, like falling off the stage into the orchestra pit. They always tell you that nobody would have noticed. Possibly, but only if they were stone dead. (**Elaine C. Smith**)

I didn't find the play remotely interesting but it went reasonably well, except for the fact that the authoress insisted on making a speech which was longer than it. (**Rikki Fulton on appearing in W.E. Gunn's *Scott of Abbotsford***)

Acting for me was a way out of being expected to be anything else. (**Richard Wilson**)

Where I came from, no one wanted to be an actor. Go and get a real job, like teaching or nursing. An actor? Who do you think you are? Stay here in the pot of lobsters with us and if you try and escape we'll pull you back in. It's this type of mentality that beats up young guys because they've got a trial with Celtic. (**Elaine C. Smith**)

My mother was in the same class as Alastair Sim, that extraordinary sinister-looking, sad-eyed actor with the voice of a fastidious ghoul, who starred in comedies like The Bells of St. Trinians, in which he played the headmistress. (**Ronnie Corbett**)

My motives in joining a drama group were anything but artistic. My girlfriend belonged to it. I reckoned there was a decent chance of losing my virginity without spending too much on bus fares. (**Brian McCardie**)

Leonardo DiCaprio is patently the result of an unnatural act of passion between William Hague and the piglet from Babe. (**A.A. Gill**)

David Carradine was found dead in a wardrobe in his Bangkok hotel room after accidentally hanging himself while attempting auto-erotic asphyxiation. The obituary said he was best known for his role as Kwai Chang Caine in the TV series *Kung Fu*. Not anymore. (**Frankie Boyle**)

I was frisked for drugs once at an airport. An official recognised me from *Trainspotting*. (**Ewan McGregor**)

ADVICE

Hegel said that at the age of fifty no man should speak for longer than he can make love. Thank you. (**Novelist Ian McEwan at an awards ceremony. This was the full extent of his speech**).

Never trust a man who, when he's alone in a room with a tea-cosy, doesn't try it on. (**Billy Connolly**)

It seldom pays to be rude. It never pays to be only half-rude. (**Norman Douglas**)

Don't vote. It only encourages them. (**Regina Craigie**)

My mother told me three things: 'Never do drugs, never marry a Catholic girl, and never be tattooed.' I went against the last one. (**Midge Ure**)

If at first you don't succeed, pry, pry again (**Philip MacDonald**)

Try and look as if you had a younger brother in Shropshire. (**J.M. Barrie giving advice to an actor in one of his plays**)

If one hides one's light under a bushel, one must be careful to point out to everyone the exact bushel under which it is hidden. (**Saki**)

The best way to rock? Just get up off your arse and wail. (**John Martyn**)

When I told my dad I was getting married, he said, 'But you're only 34 – wait another ten years.' (**Rod Stewart**)

Take more care in the toilet when you're wearing silk trousers. (**Alan Rankin**)

Let me recommend shopping to any young football player who feels they're in danger of going off the rails. It has less risk of personal injury than a punch-up outside a nightclub and you very rarely end up with a hangover. (**Brian McClair**)

The first thing a child should learn is to be a rebel. (**A.S. Neill**)

Before you judge a man, walk a mile in his shoes. After that, who cares? He's a mile away and you have his shoes. (**Billy Connolly**)

Don't go to church on Sunday and practise bayonet fighting on Monday. (**A.S. Neill**)

The best way to get a child to do something is to forbid them to do it. (**Charles Mackay**)

Love your neighbour but don't be caught. (**George Whyte-Melville**)

My great aunt, hearing that I was intending to go to London after graduating from Edinburgh University, earnestly advised me to speak only to policemen. And, if possible, exclusively to Scottish policemen. (**Iain Finlayson**)

Young boys should never be sent to bed. They'll only wake up a day older. (**J.M. Barrie**)

When in trouble, always blame the kit man. (**Brian McClair**)

Always keep Paddy behind the big mixer. (**Alfred McAlpine**)

Boss your boss as soon as you can. (**Andrew Carnegie**)

An old Scottish highlander, commending moderation in all things; commented, 'I've made twa rules a'ma life an' I've kept tae them. First, never tae drink whisky without water. Second, never tae drink water without whisky.' (**Gordon Irving**)

AGEING

My pubic hair is going grey. In a certain light you'd swear it was Stewart Granger down there. (**Billy Connolly**)

God gave us our memories so that we might have roses in December. (**J.M. Barrie**)

At my back I often hear time's winged chariot changing gear. (**Eric Linklater**)

Getting old is a bit like being drunk. Everyone else looks brilliant. (**Billy Connolly**)

We should warn against letting the golden hours slip by, even if they're only golden because we let them slip. (**J.M. Barrie**)

If I started golf earlier, I would have lost all my hair earlier – approximately by the age of 28, I would imagine. (**Sean Connery**)

Passing your 80th birthday is no great achievement. You just sit still and it happens. (**Angus McBean**)

It's no use growing older if you only learn new ways of misbehaving yourself. (**Saki**)

Thirty going on six. (**Tommy Docherty on Paul Gascoigne**)

With the fifth decade looming, women attempt to thwart the menopause by squeezing out one last baby, while men escape a sense of failure by sailing around the single-handedly, or cluttering up the drains with body parts like Denis Nielson. (**Ian Pattison**)

My psychological age is 26 and will be for many years to come. I'm told by scientific diagnosis that I should live for 200 years so I shan't be feeling middle-aged until I'm 100. (**Marie Stopes at 40**).

I've told so many lies about my age I've actually made my children illegitimate. (**Jessie Kesson**)

I knew I was getting old when I realised young people are boring. (**John Ross**)

Scott Gibbs, the 19-year-old, now 20. (**Bill McLaren**)

I know lads of twenty who are ninety, and men of sixty who are twenty. (**A.S. Neill**)

An actor, if he's clever about it, can grow old gracefully, but in the music industry you're always Peter Pan. (**Midge Ure**)

My grandfather reached a hundred and was then shot by a jealous husband. (**Finlay Currie**)

70 year old Edna Townsend has married Simon Martin, 31. I know it's an ego boost but when you go out on a date and your partner is offered a Happy Meal, maybe it's time for a re-think. (**Lorraine Kelly**)

When Mozart was my age he'd been dead for 17 years. (**Billy Connolly**)

AGGRESSION

The Liverpool theme song is *You'll Never Walk Alone*. The Wimbledon one is 'You'll Never Walk Again'. (**Tommy Docherty**)

War is hell and all that, but it has a good deal to recommend it. It wipes out all the small nuisances of peace-time. (**Ian Hay**)

Not only would I not sign him, I wouldn't let him into the ground. (**Tommy Docherty on Vinnie Jones**)

The husband was a teetotaller. There was no other woman. The conduct complained of was that he had drifted into the habit of winding up every meal by taking out his false teeth and hurling them at his wife. (**Sir Arthur Conan Doyle**).

It's a quaint Lanarkshire custom to shout obscenities at anything different. (**Elaine C. Smith**)

Tommy Smith would start a riot in a graveyard. (**Bill Shankly**)

A Highlander isn't at peace unless he's fighting. (**Proverb**)

Did you know there's a waiting list of two years to vandalise a telephone box in Glasgow? (**Arnold Brown**)

A Scotsman was attacked by a mugger. 'Your money or your wife,' said the balaclava-clad hoodlum. 'Take my wife,' said the Scotsman laconically, 'I'm saving my money for my old age.' (**F.J. O'Brien**)

Edinburgh wasn't that badly bombed in the war but Glasgow was, and sometimes the Germans bombed Edinburgh as an afterthought on the way back from Glasgow. We got the leftovers. (**Ronnie Corbett**)

Fans usually throw underwear at me when I'm on stage but one night a guy started hurling bullets. I hit him on the head with the mike stand. (**Rod Stewart**)

He's so hard he's got tattoos on his teeth. (**Jimmy Nicholl on Dave Sinclair**)

I have a tendency to only pick fights with people much bigger than me. (**Alex Kapranos**)

ALCOHOL

Sullivan is half Irish and half Scottish. One part of him wants to get drunk and the other half doesn't want to pay for it. (**Gordon McFadden**)

Wine is the drink of the gods, milk the drink of babes, tea the drink of women, and water the drink of beasts. (**John Stuart Blackie**)

If a body could just find out the exact proportion of whisky that ought to be drunk every day and keep to that, I verily trow that he might live forever and doctors and kirkyards would go out of fashion. (**James Hogg**)

If an Irishman is blessed with the ability to talk, he's kissed the Blarney Stone. If an Englishman is blessed with this ability, he's a politician. And if a Scotsman is blessed with it, he's sober. (**Dave Allen**)

McNab was once run over by a brewery lorry. It was the first time for years that the drinks had been on him. (**Des MacHale**)

You can never please your old mates when you become famous. If you don't buy 'em a drink, they think you're being tight. If you say 'A round of drinks for all the boys on me', you're being flash. (**Rod Stewart**)

Right from the start I loved everything about drink - except the taste. (**Ian Pattison**)

There are two things a Highlander likes naked and one of them is malt whisky. (**F. Marian McNeill**)

When he came to the club, all he could say in English was 'Yes', 'No' and 'Morning'. A week later he'd added 'Thank you' and 'Budweiser'. (**Hibernian boss Jim Duffy on Dusan Vrto in 1998**)

A Scotsman was wounded in a grouse-shooting accident and was given 'a wee dram' to bring him round. His first – horrified – words were 'Is that whisky you're giving me, and me unconscious?' (**Nigel Rees**)

'Huv ye given up the bevvy, Sammy?' 'Aye, wance oan the night shift. It wis the worst ten hours o' ma life.' (**Allan Morrison**)

A precocious nine-year-old enters a public house and shouts to the waitress to bring him a whisky. The waitress looks at the height of him and asks, 'Do you want to get me into trouble?' 'Maybe later,' he says, 'but get me that drink first.' (**Tom Shields**)

Jock was due to launch a ship at Clydebank today but it didn't happen. He wouldn't let go of the bottle of bubbly. (**Norman Sinclair**)

A Scot was asked if he wanted water with his whisky. 'Only if there's room,' he replied. (**Joan Bridie**)

Scotch whisky is the cure for which there is no known disease. (**John Ferguson**)

It only takes one drink to make a Scotsman drunk – usually the thirteenth. (**Chic Murray**)

I prefer being a director to an actor. You can have a drink on the opening night. (**Richard Wilson**)

He hasn't yet found out how much drink he can hold. His highwater mark for beer is somewhere in his boots. (**Ian Hay**)

When I was sixteen I walked into a pub. When I was forty-five I stepped back out again. (**Ian Pattison**)

Argument to the Scot is a vice more attractive than whisky. (**Walter Elliott**)

People may say what they like about the decay of Christianity but the religious system that produced green Chartreuse can never really die. (**Saki**)

The difference between a Scottish wedding and a Scottish wake is one less drunk. (**Ronnie Corbett**)

Here's to you, as good as you are,
And here's to me, as bad as I am;
But as good as you are, and as bad as I am,
I'm as good as you are, as bad as I am.

(**Old Scottish toast**)

Scottish people drink spasmodically and intensely for the sake of a momentary but complete release, whereas the English like to bathe and paddle about bucolically in a mild puddle of beer. (**Edwin Muir**)

It's okay for old people to drink really heavily at night. They can go up to bed on that electric chair thing attached to the staircase. (**Rhona Cameron**)

Orson Welles' idea of a balanced diet was a glass of brandy in each hand. (**Chic Murray**)

The great thing about befriending recovering alcoholics is that you're never short of a ride home. (**Billy Connolly**)

I spent all my drinking life battering people I liked and singing with my arm round people I loathed. (**Billy Connolly**)

Soccer drives you either to drink or the madhouse. And I'm not going to the madhouse. (**Tommy Docherty**)

AMBITIONS

There was a nun from the Sisters of Notre Dame whose ambition was to have her own car. After many years of saving, she managed to buy a Vauxhall Nova, and quickly became known as the Hatchback of Notre Dame. (**Tom Shields**)

The whole aim of my youthful life was to get the Bay City Rollers to fall in love with me. (**Caroline Sullivan**)

It's a really good idea to take just a couple of minutes and make a wish list of your ambitions but it should be a reasonably realistic one. On my own wish list I had to cross off being the first woman to walk on the moon and the first to win the World Cup for Scotland by scoring a hat trick against Brazil. (**Lorraine Kelly**)

My childhood desire was to kill a king. (**Andrew Carnegie**)

I want to build a team that's so invincible they'll have to send a team from Mars to beat us. (**Bill Shankly on Liverpool in 1971**)

I'd like to write a musical about drunk people and call it Liverdance. (**Billy Connolly**)

I have a great desire to make people smile, not laugh. Laughter is too aggressive. People bare their teeth. (**Muriel Spark**)

My ambition is to be on Eric Clapton's fridge door. (**Billy Connolly**)

I'd like to live on a ranch in Montana with sixteen whippets, three Arab horses, a peregrine falcon and Ann-Margret, breeding misfits like myself. (**Billy MacKenzie**)

My ambition is to go up to Agatha Christie's front door, ring the bell, wait for the butler to answer it, then shout, 'You did it!' (**Billy Connolly**)

ANIMALS

Monkeys very sensibly refrain from speech lest they should be set to earn their living. (**Kenneth Grahame**)

Every reformation must have its victims. You can't expect the fatted calf to share the enthusiasm of the angels over the prodigal's return. (**Saki**)

I don't hunt. I don't see why I should break my neck because a dog chooses to run after a nasty smell. (**Arthur J. Balfour**)

Babies are so human they remind one of monkeys. (**Saki**)

In Texas, when Orvell Lloyd was asked why he had killed his mother-in-law, he said he'd mistaken her for a raccoon. (**Richard Wilson**)

Women and elephants never forget an injury. (**Saki**)

Rabies was rumoured to have been involved as Samantha Fox was bitten by a stray cat while on holiday in Thailand. Medical staff tried everything but unfortunately the cat died. (**Frankie Boyle**)

A man said to me once, 'Do you know the Battersea Dog's Home? I replied, 'I didn't even know he was away.' (**Dave Willis**)

Who discovered that milk comes from cows? What were they doing at the time? (**Ronnie Corbett**)

The weather is so windy in the Hebrides at the moment, a chicken laid the same egg three times. (**Ian Nairn**)

Did you hear about the Scotsman who bought a black and white dog because he thought the licence would be cheaper than for a coloured one? (**Chubby Brown**)

Why did the hedgehog cross the road? To see his flat mate. (**Andy Cameron**)

Great animals, octopuses. They can pick their noses and scratch their arses at the same time. (**Billy Connolly**)

I asked the butcher if he had a wild duck. 'No, he replied, 'but I've got one I could aggravate for you.' (**Chic Murray**)

Robert Louis Stevenson was so pious he tried to convert sheep by reading passages from the Bible aloud to them. (**Karl Shaw**)

I once said to somebody, 'Did you know that 52 pigeons were given medals for bravery during the war? And a horse as well?' He replied, 'Why would a pigeon want a horse?' (**Ewan McGregor**)

My uncle had a rabbit's foot for thirty years. His other one was quite normal. (**Gordon Campbell**)

A woman who takes her husband about with her everywhere is like a cat that goes on playing with a mouse long after she's killed it. (**Saki**)

According to a recent survey, the Loch Ness monster is the world's most unexplained mystery. Or as the Scots call it: 'The weather's shit. We need something to bring in the tourists.' (**Jimmy Carr**)

APPEARANCE

I was thrilled at being voted the 5th best-looking sportsman in the world in 1990...until I learned Ivan Lendl finished above me. (**Ally McCoist**)

His face is so roomy it billows in the wind like an astronaut's at take-off. (**Ginny Dougary on Robbie Coltrane**)

What are you going to do for a face when King Kong wants his arse back? (**Stanley Baxter to a heckler at one of his shows**)

Clive James walks like a man who's just discovered there's no toilet paper. (**A.A. Gill**)

You're looking better than usual – but then that's so easy for you. (**Saki to an acquaintance**)

Roy Orbison only had two facial expressions. And both of them were the same. (**Lulu**)

Once you've seen your features reproduced in the newspaper you feel you would like to be a veiled Turkish woman for the rest of your life. (**Saki**)

Years of sorrow and of care have made his head come through his hair. (**Harry Graham**)

From the age of thirteen I was never without a boyfriend. Not because I was gorgeous but because I was relatively pretty. Well, it was Motherwell. (**Elaine C. Smith**)

The last time ah seen legs like that there was a message tied tae wan a them. (**Michael Munro on a skinny youth who tried out for a football test with him**)

He looks like a pissed vampire. (**Chris Donald on Alan Hansen**)

What first attracted me to Marilyn Monroe was the lost look in the middle of her smile. (**Photographer Bill Burnside**)

I wouldnae have plastic surgery. You cannae polish a turd. (**Sam Leith**)

BEHAVIOUR

There is nothing, absolutely nothing, half as much fun as simply messing about in boats. (**Kenneth Grahame**)

If the Scots knew enough to go indoors when it rained they'd never get any exercise. (**Simon Ford**)

If you make up a song at a drunken party, people always join in. They convince themselves they know it! (**Billy Connolly**)

Some people buy their partners. I grow my own. (**Andrew Carnegie**)

You have to open your mind to every new experience. This week I've been practising sneezing with my eyes open. (**Billy Connolly**)

The first mobile phone I bought cost £2,000. It looked like a brick with an aerial. If anyone ever called me on it I was so embarrassed I let it ring until I could find the sanctity of a phone box to answer it in. (**Midge Ure**)

It's never the last place you look if you don't look. (**John Ross**)

It's wonderful how much news there is when people write to you every day. If they wait for a month there's nothing that seems worth telling. (**O. Douglas**)

Most actors I've come across through my work are a seething mass of insecurities. Their way of feeling important is to behave like a toddler having a temper tantrum in the supermarket. (**Lorraine Kelly**)

I got up this morning. I like to get up in the morning. It gives me the rest of the day to myself. (**Chic Murray**)

BIRTH

At twelve thirty p.m. on Tuesday the fifteenth of April 1924, made my first entrance on the world stage just in time for lunch. (**Rikki Fulton**)

All the babies born in Scotland are very young. (**Allan Morrison**)

One of my patients was a childless woman aged forty and married for fifteen years, who suddenly decided that she was pregnant. She developed every sign and symptom of being so. She had morning sickness, a capacious appetite, breast changes and swelling of the abdomen. Nothing could convince her that the condition was a pure neurosis. I could only repeat Lord Asquith's famous phrase, 'Madam, we shall wait and see'. And indeed, at the end of nine months, she brought forth ... wind. (**A.J. Cronin**)

As a foetus I was an avid Rangers fan. (**Graeme Souness**)

'Granny, do storks really bring babies?'
'Of course, pet.'
'Well who brings the elephants then?'
(**Allan Morrison**)

Being born was my first big mistake. (**Robbie Coltrane**)

Possession of a Scottish birth certificate guarantees us a place in the front of the queue for death certificates. (**Gordon Smith**)

With the birth of each child you lose two novels. (**Candida MacWilliam**)

I genuinely believe I was born singing. I hope to die the same way. (**Lulu**)

The young married woman across the landing from Mrs O'Rourke had triplets the other day. She was awfully proud of her three bonnie babies. 'It's most unusual to have triplets,' she said, 'the doctor told me that it only happens once in two hundred thousand times.' 'Once in two hundred thousand times?' said Mrs O'Rourke, 'When do ye find time to do yur housework?' (**Stanley Baxter**)

I was a test-tube baby. My star sign is Pyrex. (**Rod McCowan**)

I was born in Largs on 24 August 1953. For the one and only time in my life, I was early. (**Sam Torrance**)

BOOKS

A lot of people think they can take my books and analyse me from them. On that principle, Agatha Chrsitie would be a serial killer. (**Muriel Spark**)

If his books were pop-ups, a steel-toed Doc Marten boot would lash out from every page and pulverise your face to a sticky puree of blood and powdered bone. (**Olaf Tyaransen on Irvine Welsh**)

It is all very well to write books but can you waggle your ears? (**J.M. Barrie**)

My pre-computer life was dominated by a fear of losing manuscripts. Whenever I went on holiday I used to keep them in the fridge. I read somewhere that even in Hiroshima bomb blasts a fridge could remain intact. (**William Boyd**)

Ach, any idiot can write a book. (**Alastair MacLean**)

CHILDREN AND CHILDHOOD

When the first baby laughed the first time, the laugh broke into a million pieces and they all went skipping about. That was the beginning of fairies. (**J.M. Barrie**)

Many people prefer children to dogs. Principally, I think, because a licence is not required for the former. (**Harry Graham**)

I practically lived in cinemas as a child; one night after watching Hell on Frisco Bay I fell asleep. Nobody knew I was in the seat so they locked the place up. I woke up at 4 a.m. and tried to get out. I was picked up by the police because they thought I was after breaking in! (**Brian Cox**)

Children are growing up when they stop asking you where they came from and start refusing to tell you where they're going. (**Allan Morrison**)

What's the difference between a Rottweiler and a social worker? Ye can get yer wean back off a Rottweiler. (**Michael Munro**)

We didnae have much money for laxatives as children. Our mammies just put us sittin' on the lavvy and told us ghost stories. (**Stuart Buchanan**)

I decided to become an author at the age of three. (**George MacDonald Fraser**)

As a small boy I was torn between two ambitions: to be a footballer or to run away and join a circus. At Partick Thistle I got to do both. (**Alan Hansen**)

I think she must have been strictly brought up. She's so desperately anxious to do the wrong thing correctly. (**Saki**)

I don't know how long a child will remain utterly static in front of the television but my guess is that it could be well into their thirties. (**A.A. Gill**)

The hours and years some children spent birdwatching I spent watching people. (**R.D. Laing**)

Nothing much happens after you're six years old. (**J.M. Barrie**)

I prefer acquaintances to friends. They don't expect you to go to their children's weddings. (**A.A. Gill**)

CLOTHING

If I were forced to wear a mini-skirt I'd have to see a psychiatrist. (**Annie Lennox**)

The kilt is an unrivalled garment for fornication and diarrhoea. (**John Masters**)

Sean Connery likes to dress casually. If you persuaded him to wear a suit for a business meeting you'd probably discover he had no socks on. (**Ursula Andress**)

Whenever I wear something expensive it looks stolen. (**Billy Connolly**)

Very often Rod (Stewart) chose to wear my cotton panties on stage. Not only were they more comfortable for him, they were also invisible beneath his skin-tight trousers. (**Britt Ekland**)

Her frocks are built in Paris but she wears them with a strong English accent. (**Saki**)

No, everything's in perfect working order! (**Classic Scots response to the question, 'Is anything worn under that kilt'?**)

Some people are born with a sense of how to clothe themselves, some acquire it, and others look as if their clothes had been thrust upon them. (**Saki**)

I'm moving to India because I'm fed up wearing socks. (**J.B.S. Haldane**)

I fear that the development of the railways will destroy the need for waterproof coats. (**Charles MacIntosh**)

A butterfly should be able to fly up between yourself and your dress without so much as brushing the powder from its wings. (**Marie Stopes, who liked dressing without a corset or bra**).

Put even the plainest woman into a beautiful dress and unconsciously she will try to live up to it. (**Lady Duff Gordon**)

Trying to find people who wear flares today is like trying to find people who voted for Margaret Thatcher. (**Bill Nighy**)

If Jesus Christ came back today, he and I would get into our brown corduroys and go to the nearest jean store and overturn the racks of blue denim. Then we'd get crucified in the morning. (**Ian Anderson**)

If Freud had worn a kilt in the prescribed Highland manner, he might have had a different attitude to genitals. (**Anthony Burgess**)

Recent research has shown why Scotsmen wear kilts. In 1317 Sandy McNab won a lady's tartan skirt in a raffle. (**Des MacHale**)

I took a photograph of the wife in a fawn kilt and everybody swore it was a snap of Ben Nevis. (**Les Dawson**)

At the Games, George walked proudly in full highland dress with his wife. Suddenly he whispered to her, 'What do you think those English tourists would say if I lifted my kilt and flashed my haggis at them?' His wife replied, 'They'd probably say I married you for your money.' (**Bill Shipton**)

Azinger is wearing an all-black outfit: black jumper, blue trousers, white shoes and a pink tea cosy hat. (**Renton Laidlaw**)

COMPARISONS

Wearing tight striped pants, he looked like a bifurcated marrow. (**Clive James on Rod Stewart**)

Wimbledon have [sic] as much charm as a broken beer bottle. (**Tommy Docherty**)

His moves were as sensitive as a pickpocket's hands. (**Hugh McIlvanney on George Best**)

Kenny Dalglish has about as much personality as a tennis racquet. (**Mike Channon**)

Facing a Ronald Koeman free kick is like facing a serial killer. (**Archie MacPherson**)

I remember when I first saw him he was just 13 and he floated over the ground like a cocker spaniel chasing a piece of silver paper in the wind. (**Alex Ferguson on Ryan Giggs**)

Jimmy Hill is to football what Herod was to babysitting. (**Tommy Docherty**)

He uses statistics as a drunken man uses lampposts – for support rather than illumination. (**Andrew Lang on an acquaintance**)

His flabby, redundant figure sat UP in bewildered semi-consciousness, like an ice-cream that has been taught to beg. (**Saki**)

What's the difference between a Scotsman and a canoe? A canoe sometimes tips. (**Walter Finlay**)

The whole fame thing has a strange effect on me. Not that I think I'm Demi Moore, although a lot of people have said I'm her spit, and I have to admit that we do have very similar ankles. (**Elaine C. Smith**)

The last time I saw something like that, it was crawling out of Sigourney Weaver's stomach. (**Ally McCoist on David Bowman of Dundee United**)

A page of my journal is like a cake of portable soup. A little may be diffused into a considerable portion. (**James Boswell**)

What is it that Rangers, Celtic and a three-pin plug have in common? They're all completely useless in Europe. (**Michael Munro**)

The wives of the American team at the Ryder Cup usually turn up looking like off-duty lap dancers. (**Lawrence Donegan**)

Voting Tory is like being in trouble with the police: You'd rather the neighbours didn't know. (**Charles Kennedy**)

A Glasgow man watching Arnold Palmer hit a monstrous drive during the Open at Troon turned to his wife as the ball went screaming away into the distance and said, 'Jean, that man hits the ball farther than we go on our holidays. (**James A. Simpson**)

He had a voice that reminded one of a fat bishop blessing a butter-making competition. (**Saki**)

Colin Montgomerie walks round a golf course like a man under the impression that smiling gives you herpes. (**Lawrence Donegan**)

Attending a Kenny Dalglish press conference was akin to walking into a room in which a married couple have just had a major row about sex. (**Harry Pearson**)

When a man confronts catastrophe on the road he looks in his purse. A woman looks in her mirror. (**Margaret Turnbull**)

Watching John Thaw is like being embalmed alive by an arthritic with halitosis. (**A.A. Gill**)

CONTRADICTIONS

Comedy is only comic if you play it seriously. (**Alexander Mackendrick**)

The American people are very proud of their heritage so they like it to be as modern as possible. (**Robbie Coltrane**)

The actors who try to teach you how to do it are always the ones you don't want to learn from. (**Ewan McGregor**)

She's so desperately anxious to do the wrong thing correctly, I think she must have been very strictly brought up. (**Saki**)

Addresses are given to us to conceal our whereabouts. (**Saki**)

Without picking out anyone in particular, I thought Mark Wright was tremendous. (**Graeme Souness**)

The Scottish will venture boldly to the uttermost ends of the earth, while loudly proclaiming that they wished they had never left home. (**Alastair MacLean**)

There are no winners and no losers. Everybody loses. (**Ian McGregor**)

Only an obscene person will condemn obscenity. (**A.S. Neill**)

He that has a secret to hide should not only hide it, but hide that he has it to hide. (**Thomas Carlyle**)

I am never satisfied that I have handled a subject properly until I have contradicted myself at least three times. (**John Ruskin**)

CONUNDRUMS

What do you give the man who's had everyone? (**Rod Stewart's ex Alana on the difficulty of choosing a birthday present for him**)

Lester Piggott is a volcano trapped in an iceberg. (**Hugh McIlvanney**)

If Harry Potter is so magical, why can't he cure his bad eyesight and get laid? (**Frankie Boyle**)

What is algebra exactly; is it those three-cornered things? (**J.M. Barrie**)

Is there anything in life so disenchanting as attainment? (**Robert Louis Stevenson**)

In airplanes, why is there a lifejacket under the seat instead a parachute? And why is there no window in the toilet? Who on earth is going to look in? And where do all the wee jobbies go on planes? 340 people on a Jumbo for 7½ hours – that's a lot of jobbies. (**Billy Connolly**)

Why do people look in their handkerchiefs after they blow their noses? What do they expect to find – a silver sixpence? (**Billy Connolly**)

The gaffer said at the end of his team talk, 'Has anybody got any questions?' 'Yes,' I said 'Where do babies come, from?' (**Brian McClair**)

If you're going to make a book end badly, it must end badly from the beginning. (**Robert Louis Stevenson**)

I wonder how many mice Robert Burns studied before deciding that their best-laid schemes gang aft a-gley? (**Auberon Waugh**)

How will we know it's morning if there's no servant to pull up the blinds? (**J.M. Barrie**)

Why on earth do people say things like, 'My eyes aren't what they used to be'? What did they used to be – their ears? (**Billy Connolly**)

CYNICISM

Nothing matters very much and very few things matter at all.
(**Arthur J. Balfour**)

I enjoy the excitement of working on a well-crewed picture.
It's like a microcosm of a society that really works. Because
nothing works anywhere else. (**Sean Connery**)

The greatest improvement in Scottish football over the past
ten years has been the standard of sweet trolleys at the team
get-togethers. (**Pat Nevin**)

The only thing you can believe in a newspaper is the date.
(**J.B.S. Haldane**)

What's the difference between the Scottish football team
and Roger Federer? Federer sometimes hits the net. (**Edward
Ferguson**)

While the Highlander pulls the glamour over your eyes,
the Lowlander sells you a used car. While the Lowlander
works out the bill and takes your credit card, the Highlander
persuades you it will actually go. (**Iain Finlayson**)

In Govan vocabulary there are only three adjectives: 'crap',
'shite', and, on the odd glorious occasion – say the Second
Coming or the eradication of world poverty – 'not bad'. (**Ian
Pattison**)

Set a bourgeois architect to design homes for the working
class and without fail he will design homes for sardines.
(**Alexander Trocchi**)

DATING

From my experience of life I believe my personal motto should be, 'Beware of men bearing flowers.' (**Muriel Spark**)

In my day if you took a girl out on a date, we dressed up. Now you can't even tell which sex is which. Both of them are garbed in their filthy jeans and what-have-you, doing things to each other I would have considered to be medically impossible. I said to one youth sitting on our garden wall with his tongue down his girlfriend's throat, 'If I needed to get food that badly, I'd use a tin opener.' (**Richard Wilson**)

I lost my virginity to David, my next-door neighbour. I hadn't told Alastair. I was also going out with another boy called Callum. I didn't tell Alastair about Callum or Callum about Alastair. Or either of them about David. Plus, I was still in love with Nicola Russell, who wouldn't see me anymore, and I was also going out with my first lesbian lover Josephine. I was trying to keep her under wraps too. (**Rhona Cameron**)

A Scotsman took a girl for a taxi ride. She was so beautiful he could hardly keep his eyes on the meter. (**Des MacHale**)

I remember walking a girl down a lane one evening after the cinema and thinking, 'In three lampposts' time I will take her hand', then ducking it on the third and saying, 'No, I'll make that four lampposts'. Then: 'All right, definitely after the ninth lamppost – and maybe just past that second big tree.' (**Ronnie Corbett**)

DEATH

I became a gravedigger to confront my fear of death. (**Rod Stewart**)

The ideal board of football directors should be made up of three men – two dead and the other dying. (**Tommy Docherty**)

Whenever I feel tempted to be industrious I go to Kensal Green and look at the graves of those who were. (**Saki**)

An author was once sentenced to death for murdering his publisher. When he was on the scaffold he saw some other publishers in the front row. He didn't say goodbye to them. He just said, 'I'll see you later.' (**J.M. Barrie**)

Not too long ago I lay awake in bed and counted all the people I've known who died racing. The final count was 57. (**Jackie Stewart**)

'Hey, Gerry,' exclaimed the foreman, 'Dae you believe in life after death?' 'Aye,' replied Gerry, 'ah dae'.'Well ah'm awfa pleased,' said the foreman. 'Yesterday, jist efter the lunch break, when you left tae go tae yer friend Billy's funeral, he came intae the yard looking fur a start.' (**Allan Morrison**)

If you gave a Scotsman poison, he wouldn't die until he got his deposit back on the bottle. (**Les Dawson**)

The old Scots lady lay dying. She looked up and asked her husband if he would do her just one small favour before she went. 'John,' she said, 'on the day o' the funeral I'd like ye tae ride in the same coach as ma mother'. John replied, 'A'richt Janet. I'll dae that tae please ye. But 'twill completely spoil the day for me.' (**Gordon Irving**)

Family tradition has it that Sir Thomas Urquhart's death was caused by an uncontrollable fit of laughter on hearing of the Restoration of Charles II. (**Catherine Caufield**)

I've made my wife promise to put 'Jesus Christ – is it that time already?' on my tombstone. (**Billy Connolly**)

I was editor of the Sunday Times a full hour before I received my first death threat. (**Andrew Neil**)

I'd like to die by failing off a bar stool in a nightclub. (**Billy MacKenzie**)

When we scored our equaliser, I patted Jock (Stein) on the head but he just sat motionless. He was gone but I didn't realise it. My thoughts were totally absorbed in a stupid game of football. (**Alex Ferguson**)

Audiences sometimes love you to death – literally. Look what happened to John Lennon. (**Donovan**)

The wording I want on my tombstone is, 'Count as long as you like – I'm not getting up this time.' (**Former world boxing champion Jim Watt**)

I'd hate to die with a good liver, good kidneys and a good brain. When I die I want everything to be knackered. (**Hamish Imlach**)

My wife's great grandfather was killed at Custer's Last Stand. He didn't actually take part in the fighting. He was camping nearby and went over to complain about the noise. (**Ronnie Corbett**)

DEDICATION

When I'm having sex I try to do my nine times tables to make it last longer. I once got to 'Eight nines are seventy-two', and did a lap of honour round the bed. (**Billy Connolly**)

When I started writing I spent hours looking for an adjective. I corrected and re-corrected until the page looked like a spider's web. Then I tore it up and started again. (**A.J. Cronin**)

The true artist has no interest in his work when it is finished. No work of art ever pleases its creator. His aim is perfection. (**A.S. Neill**)

You can be motoring into work and you see a bunch of kids laughing in the street. The first instinct that flashes through your mind is: You can't be laughing; Manchester United lost last night. (**Alex Ferguson**)

I've got no time for shirkers. I want a man who'll go through a wall of fire, break a leg, and still come out shooting for goal. (**Bill Shankly**)

I have no interest in gardening. If I did I'd probably plant my flowers in a 4-4-2 formation. (**Tommy Docherty**)

DEFINITIONS

We hear war called murder. It is not – it is suicide. (**Ramsay Macdonald**)

Exhaustion is the breeding-ground of procrastination. (**William Boyd**)

Autobiography is an attempted jail-break. (**Stuart Hood**)

A film set is a never-ending hell. (**Tom Conti**)

Fishing is something between a sport and a religion. (**Josephine Tey**)

Insanity is a perfectly rational adjustment to an insane world. (**R.D. Laing**)

Kevin Keegan is the Julie Andrews of football. (**Duncan McKenzie**)

A silly, transparent coxcomb. (**J.G. Lockhart on Samuel Pepys**)

Dogma is the collective wisdom of individual ignorance. (**Thomas Carlyle**)

Boats are just holes in the water that you throw money into. (**Midge Ure**)

Horse sense is the instinct that keeps horses from betting on humans. (**Josephine Tey**)

The Zombie with the Crombie. (**Archie McCulloch on Rikki Fulton**)

A diary is an assassin's cloak which we wear when we stab someone in the back with a pen. (**William Soutar**)

A diplomat is somebody who can tell you to go to hell and leave you looking forward to the trip. (**Alex Salmond**)

Fishing is transcendental meditation with a punchline. (**Billy Connolly**)

DISGUST

If Everton were playing down at the bottom of my garden, I'd draw the curtains. (**Bill Shankly**)

James Bond is a cross, a privilege, a joke, a challenge … and as bloody intrusive as a nightmare. (**Sean Connery**)

The same old sausage, fizzing and spluttering in its own grease. (**Henry James on Thomas Carlyle**)

Smoking is a custom loathsome to the eye, hateful to the nose, harmful to the brain, dangerous to the lungs, and in the black, stinking fume thereof, nearest resembling the horrible Stygian smoke of the pit that is bottomless. (**King James 1**)

A hoary-beaded, toothless baboon. (**Thomas Carlyle on Ralph Waldo Emerson**)

Carlyle is a poet to whom nature has destroyed the faculty of verse. (**Alfred Lord Tennyson**)

Thackeray settled like a meat-fly on whatever one had got for dinner, and made one sick of it. (**John Ruskin**)

He was not only over-filled with learning, but stood in the slop. (**Thomas Carlyle on Lord Macaulay**)

EDUCATION

The clever men at Oxford
Knew all there is to be knowed
But none of them know half as much
As intelligent Mr Toad.
(**Kenneth Grahame**)

Having no education, I had to use my brain. (**Bill Shankly**)

Experience teaches us that it doesn't. (**Norman MacCaig**)

Lack of education is an extreme handicap when one is being offensive. (**Josephine Tey**)

Teaching drives a man to either drink, golf or insanity. (**John Muir**)

It's the educated barbarian who's the worst. He knows what to destroy. (**Helen MacInnes**)

The happiest time of my school life was every day at four o'clock when the bell went. (**Jackie Stewart**)

Don't enforce music or maths on unwilling children. Young Freddy Beethoven and young Tommy Einstein will refuse to be kept away from their respective spheres in time. (**A.S. Neill**)

In Aston Villa there was a feeling that too much education was bad for your legs. (**Brian McClair**)

I shall never be sure whether I was never any good at Geography because I disliked my Geography teacher or whether I disliked my Geography teacher because I was never any good at Geography. (**R.D. Laing**)

My favourite subject at school was rugby, followed closely by rugby. (**Bill McLaren**)

The teacher brought the belt down with unbelievable force on me but as he did so I disengaged my hands. He yelled with pain as he inadvertently belted his own private parts and almost castrated himself. (**Rikki Fulton**)

My wife is a classy girl. All her tattoos are spelt right. (**Chic Murray**)

The school I went to was tough I was expelled for not smoking. (**Tommy Henderson**)

Concerned granny to eleven-year-old grandson: 'Were the examination questions awfa' hard? 'No, Granny, they were OK. It was the answers that were difficult.' (**Allan Morrison**)

Glasgow students have their own rhyming slang for a lower second class honours degree, or two-two as it is known in academic circles. It is called a Desmond, after the well-known South African bishop. (**Tom Shields**)

I was so useless at algebra it took me ten minutes to realise the test paper was upside down. For all I knew, The Equations could have been a 50s rock'n'roll band. (**Andy Cameron**)

EGOTISM

If Graeme Souness was a chocolate-drop he'd eat himself. (**Archie Gemmill**)

In one year I travelled 450,000 miles by air. That's about 18½ times around the world – or once round Howard Cosell's head. (**Jackie Stewart**)

When I was at the peak of my career I could fart in a bathtub and still be number one. (**Rod Stewart**)

Of what is interesting in Scottish writing in the past twenty years or so, I have written it all. (**Alexander Trocchi**)

Utopia could be reached in my lifetime had I the power to issue inviolable edicts. (**Marie Stopes**)

He once made history by going almost a minute without mentioning the fact that he was once signed for Liverpool. (**Ally McCoist on Alex Totton**)

I consider the world as made for me, not me for the world. It is my maxim therefore to enjoy it while I can and let futurity shift for itself. (**Tobias Smollett**)

An American who had been touring Scotland in the company of a Scottish relative had been persistently belittling everything he saw. On the return journey to Edinburgh, he glimpsed the Forth Rail Bridge. 'What's that?' he asked. Back came the reply, 'I don't know, but it wasn't there last week.' (**James Simpson**)

I will be canonised in 200 years' time. (**Marie Stopes**)

We shouldn't spend hours on end examining our navels and becoming so self-obsessed that we're in danger of disappearing up our own backsides. (**Lorraine Kelly**)

ENGLAND AND THE ENGLISH

In England, Scotland is considered almost a foreign country. (**Piers Morgan**)

What would Scotland be like without soccer? England. (**Tony Higgins**)

The day England won the World Cup was the blackest day of my life. (**Denis Law**)

The English are better at laughing at themselves than the Scots. But then they have more to laugh about. (**Matt McGinn**)

An Englishmen's real ambition is to find a railway carriage to himself. (**Ian Hay**)

Englishmen think over a compliment for a week so that by the time they pay it, it is addled like a bad egg. (**W.J. Locke**)

We know no spectacle so ridiculous as the British public in one of its periodical fits of morality. (**Lord Macaulay**)

A Scotsman who was staggered at the size of the dinner bill in a London hotel said to the waiter, 'If you English had charged liked this at Bannockburn, you might have won.' (**James Simpson**)

Part of the joy of being Scottish is not being English. (**Hugh MacDiarmid**)

England, these days, is like a drunk tumbling home from the pub on a Friday night. Scotland is the nagging wife. (**Ian Pattison**)

A Scots mist will wet an Englishman to the skin. (**Allan Ramsay**)

There are only three things I have against living in Britain: the place, the climate and the people. (**James Edmond**)

After Andy Murray lost at Wimbledon he went back to being called Scottish by the commentators. (**Frankie Boyle**)

Cricket is a game which the English, not being a spirited people, have invented to give themselves some conception of eternity. (**Lord Mancroft**)

A Scottish funeral is merrier than an English holiday. (**Bill Nighy**)

My father used to say that the reason the sun never set on the British Empire is because God would never trust the British in the dark. (**George Galloway**)

EXTREMES

An Iowa woman once took five years to type out all the numbers from one to a million after her son's teacher said it wasn't possible. (**Richard Wilson**)

Some people think football is a matter of life and death. It's much more important than that. (**Bill Shankly**)

If you want to be in a pop group, you either become completely debauched and die of a drug overdose after a couple of years or else you renounce everything and live like a nun. I've straddled them both. (**Annie Lennox**)

Is George Mair a conscientious journalist? Well he once telephoned a semi-colon from Moscow. (**James Bone**)

I've always liked late starters. I've seen quite a few bright children who could recite Milton at four blossom forth as drunkards-and loafers at twenty-four. (**A.S. Neill**)

FAILURE

The most vulnerable area for goalies is between their legs. (**Andy Gray**)

We don't use a stopwatch to judge our Golden Goal competition now. We use a calendar. (**Tommy Docherty on Wolves in 1985**)

Recession is when you tighten your belt. Depression is when you have no belt to tighten. When you've lost your trousers as well, you're in the airline business. (**Sir Adam Thompson**)

For years I used to think 'Partick Thistle Nil' was the name of a football team. (**Billy Connolly**)

We ended up playing football, and that doesn't suit us. (**Former Airdrie manager Alex Macdonald**)

Estate agents are people who didn't make it as second hand car salesmen. (**Billy Connolly**)

If Kitchener was not a great man he was, at least, a great poster. (**Margot Asquith**)

No one lives the perfect lifestyle. Kate Winslet is airbrushed, Cameron Diaz has spots and Nicole Kidman has spent hours in the ladies' loo at a glittering premiere suffering from anxiety attacks. (**Lorraine Kelly**)

Sandy Ferguson, for many years the barman at the Rogano and Buttery oyster bars in Glasgow, told us he had only one dissatisfied customer in all that time. He was a chap who came in and had six oysters because he had heard of their aphrodisiac properties. He phoned later to complain that one of them hadn't worked. (**Tom Shields**)

There's nothing more depressing than a chirpy loser. (**Ian Pattison**)

FAME

I'd rather have people weep at my funeral than to be famous. (**Robbie Coltrane**)

Fame is rot; daughters are the thing. (**J.M. Barrie**)

One of the hard facts of life about living in Scotland is that the public don't like winners. (**Stephen Hendry**)

Fame is being asked to sign your autograph on the back of a cigarette packet. (**Billy Connolly**)

Everyone is famous for something. I'm famous for living opposite George Bernard Shaw. (**J.M. Barrie**)

I wouldn't mind getting 2½ minutes of Andy Warhol's fifteen. (**Billy MacKenzie**)

As a general rule, a liberal dose of madness, a modicum of talent and a huge ego, coupled with massive self-doubt, seem to be the lethal ingredients necessary for the heady cocktail of fame. (**Elaine C. Smith**)

A celebrity today is a person who gives an exclusive to one publication, orchestrated by his public relations person. Then he goes off to the Caribbean and buys a yacht, and when he comes back no one knows who he is. (**Harry Benson**)

There must be something wrong in me or I wouldn't be so popular. (**Robert Louis Stevenson**)

The bigger the entourage a star has in their wake, the bigger the pain in the backside they'll be. (**Lorraine Kelly**)

FILMS AND FILM-MAKING

In Hollywood there's a simple equation to explain the constant flirtation between actors and politicians. Actors know that everyone likes them but nobody takes them seriously. Politicians know that everybody takes them seriously but nobody likes them. (**James Bone**)

The only piece of direction Alfred Hitchcock gave me on the set of Marnie was when I was listening to what somebody was saying in a scene with my mouth open, as I often do, and he thought it would look better shut. (**Sean Connery**)

I'd sooner have a writing credit on a swashbuckler than Citizen Kane. (**George MacDonald Fraser**)

An associate producer is the only one who'll associate with a producer. (**Chic Murray**)

Roman Polanski is too near the ground to be sanitary. (**John Fraser**)

Acting is travelling 1,500 miles to a foreign country to pretend to be someone else in front of a machine. (**Robbie Coltrane**)

My father was a film-maker. He always said he wanted to go like Humphrey Jennings, the legendary director who stepped backwards over a cliff while framing a shot. (**A.A. Gill**)

The reason I didn't produce Brigadoon in Scotland was because when I went there I found nothing that looked like Scotland. (**Arthur Freed**)

Film-making belongs, like all show business, to that magical world in which two and two can make five, but also three and even less. (**John Grierson**)

John Garfield entered rooms as if he were challenging their contents. (**William McIlvanney**)

I would rather take a bath in pig manure than see this film. (**Official of the Church of Scotland on *The Exorcist***)

Ancient Rome meant two things to Hollywood: Cleopatra and walking mummies. (**George MacDonald Fraser**)

Al Pacino plays a Scottish immigrant in Revolution, but every time he opens his mouth he sounds like Chico Marx with a head cold. (**Vincent Canby**)

FOOD

At acting school I was asked to think of some childhood trauma to get into a Method mood for a class. All I could come up with, buried deep in my subconscious, was the rather unenthralling tale of losing a Fry's Chocolate Cream on a river bank when I was two years old. (**Ewan McGregor**)

I can't resist ordering Brussels sprouts in restaurants because the words sound so lovely but I never eat them. (**J.M. Barrie**)

Oats is a grain which in England is generally given to horses. In Scotland supports the people. (**Dr Samuel Johnson**)

Many's the long night I've dreamed of cheese – toasted, mostly. (**Robert Louis Stevenson**)

I once scandalised a woman by declaring that clear soup was a more important factor in life than a clear conscience. (**Saki**)

Each day we dig our own graves with our teeth. (**Samuel Smiles**)

He was a very valiant man who first adventured on the eating of oysters. (**James I**)

Ferguson found himself in London with only sixpence left in his purse. He was starving and could see that a fine fish supper could be his for nine pence. He pawned the sixpence for five pence and sold the pawn ticket for four pence. (**Jimmy Logan**)

Bible-thumpers are bumping their gums about the plot of The Da Vinci Code being riddled with 'factual inaccuracies'. A bit rich, don't you think, from the same people who insist it's possible to feed 5,000 people with a packet of fish fingers and a Warburtons. (**Tam Cowan**)

A Scottish breakfast consists of a pound of steak, a bottle of whisky and a large Alsatian dog. The dog is to eat the steak. (**Des MacHale**)

The bread tasted as if it had been made by a manic depressive creative therapy class. (**A.A. Gill**)

I'm now on a banana and seaweed diet. It hasn't improved my football but I'm a helluva better swimmer. (**Gordon Strachan**)

You can't think rationally on an empty stomach, and a whole lot of people can't do it on a full one either. (**Lord Reith**)

Granny to Susan, aged four. 'Eat up your broccoli: it will put colour in your cheeks.' 'But Granny, I don't want green cheeks.' (**Allan Morrison**)

There's an old and oft-repeated joke about a young man in a Glasgow restaurant who is asked by the waiter if he would like ginger with his melon. He replies that he'll stick to the red wine, the same as the rest of the company. (**Tom Shields**)

We were so poor that on a cold night my father used to suck a peppermint and we all sat around his tongue. (**Ronnie Corbett**)

One often yearns
For the land of Burns.
The only snag is
The Haggis.
(**Lils Emslie**)

Why do people say 'You just want to have your cake and eat it'? What's the point of having a cake unless you're going to eat it? (**Billy Connolly**)

Ostrich tastes like the product of an uncomfortable liaison between a duck and a sheep. (**A.A. Gill**)

FOOTBALL

I often regret that some players don't sit in chairs fitted with a lie detector and an ejector seat. (**Gordon Strachan**)

The only thing that has never changed in the history of football is the shape of the ball. (**Denis Law**)

Robert Maxwell's just bought Brighton and Hove Albion. He's furious that it's only one club. (**Tommy Docherty in 1988**)

Too big to be a wee club and too wee to a big club. (**John Rafferty on Clyde**)

The tune began changing when the Peruvians, a goal down, suddenly revealed an ability to run faster with the ball than the Scots could run without it. (**Clive James on the 1978 World Cup**)

Is acne an occupational hazard for football strikers, as in 'Duncan Ferguson picked his spot before tucking the ball away? (**Tom Shields**)

McTavish: 'I hear you went over to Aberdeen to see the match last Saturday. Was it a big gate?' MacDonald: 'It was for sure. One of the biggest I've ever climbed over.' (**Edward Phillips**)

I support two teams: Scotland and whoever's playing England. (**Donald Cameron**)

Scotland has the only football team in the world that does a lap of disgrace. (**Billy Connolly**)

Players today spend more on a round of drinks than we were getting for a week's wages. (**Jock Stein**)

Bringing the game into disrepute is a wonderfully silly expression. It's the offender, not the game, that's disreputable. (**George MacDonald Fraser**)

Scottish football reporters are only fans with typewriters. (**J.L. Manning**)

When Jim McLean told you to sit down you didn't look around for the chair. I've seen him reduce hardened pros to tears at half-time with the kind of harangue that would leave the paint peeling off the walls. (**Andy Gray**)

Nobody ever won a tackle with a smile on his face. (**Bruce Rioch**)

The Scottish football fan's ability to smuggle drink into matches makes Papillion look like an amateur. (**Patrick Murray**)

Kenny Dalglish wasn't that big but he had a huge arse that came down below his knees. That's where he got his strength from. (**Brian Clough**)

What's the difference between Scotland and a tea-bag? Answer: A tea-bag stays longer in the cup! (**Internet joke**)

Some teams are so negative they should be sponsored by Kodak. (**Tommy Docherty**)

FOOTBALL MANAGERS

Celtic manager David Hay still has a fresh pair of legs up his sleeve. (**John Greig**)

The easiest team for a manager to pick is the Hindsight Eleven. (**Craig Brown**)

I have come to the conclusion that nice men do not take the kept managers. (**Graeme Souness**)

Kevin Keegan and I have 63 international caps between us. He has the 63. (**Craig Brown**)

A manager must buy cheap and sell dear. If someone rings to ask me about a player I'll say 'He's great, super lad, goes to church twice a day. Good in the air, two lovely feet, make a great son-in-law.' You never tell them he couldn't trap a bag of cement. (**Tommy Docherty**)

Where did it all go wrong for us? It was quite simple really. At the back, in midfield and up front. (**George Graham after a defeat**)

Berti Vogts is the most unpopular visitor to Scotland since Rudolph Hess crash-landed there! (**The Guardian**)

If you can imagine spending five years with an overgrown child clambering about in your attic then you'll have a fair idea of the impact Graeme Souness has made on Scottish football. (**Graham McColl**)

I tend to buy family men. With a married player you generally know he's at home of an evening watching *Coronation Street*. (**Bruce Rioch**)

Ron Atkinson told me early on that if I was serious about football management I'd have to get used to being sacked. (**Andy Gray**)

Arsene Wenger and Alex Ferguson don't conduct post-match pleasantries as a general rule. The Arsenal manager would, however, be happy to crack open a bottle of red with his Manchester United counterpart – provided he could use the Scot's head as a corkscrew. (**Andrew Fifield**)

FOREIGNERS

The Brazilians aren't as good as they used to be, or as they are now. (**Kenny Dalglish**)

Italians are distinguished by their disrespect for speed limits and preference for flair over civil obedience. (**Jackie Stewart**)

The people of Crete unfortunately make more history than they can consume locally. (**Saki**)

I asked a man if he was a pole vaulter. 'No,' he replied, 'I'm a German. And how did you know my name was Walter?' (**Jack Anthony**)

Even at sea, the Americans drive on the wrong side of the road. (**Rikki Fulton**)

There was a famous Clootie City costermonger who was regularly heard to cry: 'Genuine Spanish onions – none of your foreign muck here!' (**Tom Shields**)

FRIENDSHIP

The only reason I visit my friends is so I can look over my library. (**Sir Walter Scott**)

The families of one's friends are always a disappointment. (**Norman Douglas**)

To find a friend one must close an eye. To keep him two. (**Norman Douglas**)

Marriage is a sort of friendship recognised by the police. (**Robert Louis Stevenson**)

Two people can love each other without necessarily being friends. (**Mary Ure**)

If you have four friends in life you're lucky. That's as many as it takes to carry a coffin. (**Alex Ferguson**)

GAFFES

Whoever wins today will win the championship no matter who wins. (**Denis Law**)

Walsall have given City more than one anxious moment among many anxious moments. (**Denis Law**)

Isn't Halle Berry beautiful? I have a film I'd like to be in her with. I mean with her in. (**Ewan McGregor**)

Let's not talk about a bumpy pitch at this level. (**Lawrie McMenemy**)

The first half was end-to-end stuff. The second half, in contrast, was one end to the other. (**Lou Macari**)

Who should be there at the far post but yours truly, Alan Shearer. (**Colin Hendry**)

Socrates died from an overdose of wedlock. (**John G. Muir**)

Coffee isn't my cup of tea. (**Jimmy Logan**)

Batista gets most of his goals with the ball. (**Ian. St. John**)

There's no way Ryan Giggs is another George Best. He's another Ryan Giggs. (**Denis Law**)

As our regular listeners know, Christmas has come and gone. (**Duncan Cameron**)

The game is finely balanced with Celtic well on top. (**John Greig**)

Leeds have only had one shot on target. That may well have been the goal. (**Andy Gray**)

Mirandinha will have more shots this afternoon than both sides put together. (**Malcolm McDonald**)

That tie is a potential potato skin. (**Alan Hansen**)

When I say that Alex Ferguson needs to stand up and be counted, I mean that he needs to sit down and take a good look at himself in the mirror. (**Gary Mabbutt**)

The only time Nick Faldo opens his mouth is to change feet. (**David Feherty**)

When it comes to the David Beckhams of the world, this guy's up there with Roberto Carlos. (**Duncan McKenzie**)

England have the best fans in the world and Scotland's ones are also second to none. (**Kevin Keegan**)

Look at Stephen Hendry sitting there, totally focussed, just staring into space. (**David Vine**)

I watched the game and I saw an awful lot of it. (**Andy Gray**)

As with every young player, he's only eighteen. (**Alex Ferguson**)

That's the kind of goal he normally knocks in in his sleep with his eyes closed. (**Archie McPherson**)

The advantage of being at home is very much with the home side. (**Denis Law**).

It's a shame half-time came as early as it did. (**Gordon Durie**)

David Seaman isn't great when he's got to kick the ball with his feet. (**Alan Hansen**)

And tonight we have the added ingredient of Kenny Dalglish not being here. (**Martin Tyler**)

There's nothing happier than a sad Scot on Hogmanay. (**Lynn Ferguson**)

A message was once sent in wartime where the first person said, 'Send reinforcements, we're going to advance'. When it reached the end it had become, 'Send three or four pence, we're going to a dance'. (**George Galloway**)

Jon Bland didn't appear as cool as he looked. (**Renton Laidlaw**)

Give him his head and he'll take it with both hands, or feet. (**Bobby Gould**)

He was in a no-win situation unless he won. (**Murdo McLeod**)

Playing another side could be an omen but I don't believe in omens. (**George Graham**)

It was one of those goals that's invariably a goal. (**Denis Law**)

He's had two cruciates and a broken ankle. That's not easy. Every player attached to the club is praying the boy gets a break. (**Alex Ferguson on Wes Brown**)

The fans like to see Balde wear his shirt on his sleeve. (**Kenny Dalglish**)

It's a conflict of parallels. (**Alex Ferguson**)

It's one of the greatest goals ever, but I'm surprised that people are talking about it being the goal of the season. (**Andy Gray**)

There will be more football in a moment, but first we've got the highlights of the Scottish League Cup Final. (**Gary Newbon**)

Chris Kirkland's future is definitely in front of him. (**Andy Gray**)

We're fourth in the table - fourth! I'm going home to sit with a bottle of Coke and a packet of crisps and stare at the league table on teletext for three hours. (**Gordon Strachan**)

Without picking out anyone in particular, I thought Mark Wright was tremendous. (**Graeme Souness**)

This is the earliest I've ever been late. (**Ally McCoist**)

Alasdair McNeane was a man possessed of such consuming eagerness that he had a habit of reacting to remarks that had not yet been made. (**John Preston**)

GLASGOW

The difference between the Glasgow Mafia and the Edinburgh Mafia is that the Edinburgh Mafia make you an offer you can't refuse and the Glasgow Mafia make you one you can't understand. (**Allan Morrison**)

You can have more fun at a Glasgow funeral than at an Edinburgh wedding. (**Ian Strachan**)

The great thing about Glasgow now is that if there's a nuclear attack, it'll look exactly the same afterwards. (**Billy Connolly**)

A Glaswegian atheist is a bloke who goes to a Rangers-Celtic match to watch the football. (**Sandy Strang**)

In Glasgow, even if you couldn't afford to eat, you always wore the right clothes. (**Lulu**)

They serve a drink in Glasgow called the Souness – one half and you're off. (**Tommy Docherty**)

Of course I don't mind the fight being at three in the morning. Everyone in Glasgow fights at three in the morning. (**Boxer Jim Watt**)

The trouble with Freud is that he never played the Glasgow Empire Saturday night. (**Les Dodd**)

Even if you live in Castlemilk or Haghill you're still a Glaswegian and you swagger about thinking you're great. Unfortunately if you come from Motherwell the only thing you've got to swagger about is that at least it's not Coatbridge. (**Elaine C. Smith**)

The state of deprivation in Glasgow is appalling. There's a waiting list of two years to vandalise a phone box. (**Arnold Brown**)

You must not look down on Glasgow. It gave the world the internal combustion engine, political economy, antiseptic surgery, the balloon, the mariner's compass, the theory of Latent Heat, Tobias Smollett ... and me. (**James Bridie**)

I was heckled once in Glasgow. I took that as a positively warm reception. If they love you there, they let you live. (**Charles Kennedy**)

In Edinburgh they regard Glasgow as a trollop of a town: brash, noisy and vulgar. The Glaswegians retaliate with their view of the typical Edinburgher: 'All fur coat and nae knickers'. (**David Ross**)

In Glasgow we've always enjoyed the ancient ceremony of throwing teetotallers into pubs on Saturday nights. (**Arnold Brown**)

A Scotsman on holiday in Iraq was giving directions to a friend on how to get to his hotel. 'It's situated about ten miles on the Glasgow side of Baghdad,' he told him. (**Des MacHale**)

'Can ye tell me how t' get to Glasgow?' the tourist enquired of the Highlander. 'Och,' the mountainy man replied, 'ye shouldnae be startin' from here.' (**Doug McFarland**)

How do you spot a Glaswegian intellectual? When he chooses 'Delilah' on a karaoke machine it's the Alex Harvey version he prefers. (**Michael Munro**)

Glasgow – the vomit of a cataleptic commercialism. (**Lewis Grassic Gibson**)

A Scotsman died and, as he thought, ascended to celestial realms. 'Heaven isn't much better than Glasgow,' he remarked, looking round at the chaos around him. 'This isn't heaven,' said he of the cloven hoof. (**Gordon Whiting**)

I'm not saying my act died in the Glasgow Empire, but an undertaker in the audience threw a tape measure at me, and some embalming fluid. (**Les Dawson**)

Glasgow isn't a melting pot. It's closer to a chip pan in which you've attempted to boil cream. (**Tom Lappin**)

GOLF

The reason Scotsmen are so good at golf is they realise that the fewer times they strike the ball, the longer it will last. (**Herbert Prochnow**)

All I've got against golf is that it takes you so far from the clubhouse. (**Eric Linklater**)

My golfing career? On one hole I'm like Arnold Palmer and then at the next I'm Lilli Palmer. (**Sean Connery**)

Golf was invented by the Scottish to allow them to make meaningless Celtic noises from the back of the throat. (**Stephen Fry**)

Pinero has finished the putt. I wonder what he's thinking in Spanish. (**Renton Laidlaw**)

When golf first started, one under par was a birdie, two under par was an eagle and three under par was a partridge. They had to change that because you can't get a partridge on a par three. (**John MacKay**)

Golf is a game in which grown men and women flog, flail and fracture a green landscape on which 18 holes are hidden in satanic design. (**James Simpson**)

Andy Cameron is the only guy I know who could write 'Merry Christmas' with his backswing. (**Stevie Bree**)

Colin Montgomerie couldn't count his balls and get the same answer twice. (**David Feherty**)

The Scots invented golf. Which could also explain why they invented Scotch. (**James Dent**)

Golf is as Scottish as haggis, cockie-leekie, high cheekbones and rowanberry jam. (**Andrew Lang**)

The fact that I didn't win an eighth Order of Merit title was probably what saved my marriage. (**Colin Montgomerie**)

As for the event held annually in Augusta, Georgia – what's so great about flowerbeds and misogyny? (**Lawrence Donegan**)

Good swing? My God, mon, Joyce Wethered could hit a ball 240 yards on the fly while standing barefoot on a cake of ice. (**Willie Wilson**)

Golf in Scotland? Of course. The only other thing you can do over there is wear a skirt. (**George Low**)

HEALTH AND INJURY

This Scottish fellow had a hip replacement operation. He asked the surgeon if he could have the bone for the dog. (**Frank Carson**)

The doctor phoned his patient and said, 'I have some good news and some bad news for you, Hamish. The good news is that they're going to name a disease after you.' (**Allan Morrison**)

Leeds United are having problems with injuries. The players keep recovering. (**Bill Shankly**)

John Barnes' problem is that he gets injured appearing on *A Question of Sport*. (**Tommy Docherty**)

I can't imagine Tomas Brolin jumping for a ball. One of his eyelashes might fall out. (**George Graham on the injury-prone player**)

In Govan, until something actually turns black and drops off, they think its bad form to bother the doctor. (**Rab C. Nesbitt**)

I've had so many stitches that if I shaved my hair off, my head would look like a knitted balaclava. (**John Martin**)

I daren't play in a five-aside at Anfield. If I collapsed no one would give me the kiss of life. (**Graeme Souness after he had open heart surgery in 1993**)

He needed five stitches, three in the first half and two at the interval when his brain started to seep through. (**Alex Ferguson on Steve Bruce after he was injured in a match in 1963**)

I had butterflies in my stomach so I went to the doctor. He asked me if I'd eaten anything recently. 'Yes,' I told him, 'Butterflies.' (**Lex McLean**)

I was ill a lot as a child. I had more blood tests than they do in a week at the Mayo Clinic. I'd run a temperature at the drop of a hat. Most of it was psychosomatic. I wanted to find any way I could to avoid going to school. (**Jackie Stewart**)

Then there was the football fan who sued a Scottish league club because he was injured while watching a match. He fell out of the tree beside the grounds. (**Jim McTaig**)

Scottish football players are more prone to injury than any others. Derek Dougan said there are three questions old players always ask each other when they meet up: 'Are you still with the wife?', 'Have you got any grandchildren?' and 'How's the knee?' (**Andy Gray**)

I had to go to the doctor for a medical. Is there anything worse than handing a jar of warm piss to an attractive woman? (**Billy Connolly**)

After many attempts, I've concluded that it's impossible to eat a Toblerone without injuring yourself. (**Billy Connolly**)

IGNORANCE ·

Dad's knowledge of what goes on outside football is so restricted that he couldn't understand why he kept getting into trouble for parking on double yellow lines. He thought they were a new form of street decoration. (**Tommy Docherty's daughter Catherine Lockley**)

When I signed Jim Holton from Shrewsbury for £100,000, Harry Gregg told me I had a player who didn't know the meaning of the word defeat. I told him defeat wasn't the only word he didn't understand. There was also pass, control, dribble... (**Tommy Docherty**)

Some Glaswegians have only a tenuous grasp of our glorious past. I was reminded of this when a friend reported overhearing this remark in a pub: 'What Scotland needs today is a great leader. It's time we had another Wallace the Bruce!' (**Michael Munro**)

A lot of my players think Manual Labour is the Spanish president. (**Tommy Docherty**)

IMAGE

The problem with interviews of this sort is to get across the fact that, without breaking your arse, one is not Bond, one was functioning reasonably well before Bond, and that one is going to function reasonably well after Bond. (**Sean Connery to a reporter who identified him as that character in 1965**)

When I was young I was portrayed as the epitome of the swinging chick who dated handsome guys. In reality I felt like the last remaining virgin in London. (**Lulu**)

For years I've been a bad manic-depressive but people don't see that in me because I can only do what I do when I'm feeling pretty up. If I'm down, I'm under the bedclothes. (**Annie Lennox**)

I like Sidney Lumet's comment: 'I know Paul Newman isn't a legend because I go to the toilet with him.' (**Sean Connery**)

Ever since *Harry Potter* I've become a role model. That means I have to stop being thrown out of nightclubs at two in the morning. (**Robbie Coltrane**)

INJUSTICE

For Manchester United to get a penalty we need a certificate from the Pope and a personal letter from the Queen. (**Alex Ferguson**)

When one has been threatened with a great injustice, one accepts a smaller one as a favour. (**Jane Welsh Carlyle**)

No one ever writes about the clever little twists that I put into my songs. All they're concerned about is the women in my life, how much I drink and how much money I've got. (**Rod Stewart**)

I've seen harder tackles in the pie queue at half-time than the ones punished in games. (**Former Falkirk chairman George Fulston on over-strict referees**)

If I was in Hollywood I would be applauded for wearing hacket clothes, a bad wig and no make-up. Robert De Niro puts on weight and bad make-up and gets nominated for an Oscar. What do I get? Two guys hanging out of a bread van shouting 'Hello, Mary Doll'. (**Elaine C. Smith**)

I once gave a performance which drew a frosty response from a lady in the front row. She said to me afterwards, 'Yon's a grand wee comedian – a had an awfy job tae keep frae laughin'.' (**Sir Harry Lauder**)

INTELLIGENCE

The powers of a man's mind are directly proportional to the quantity of coffee he drinks. (**Sir James Mackintosh**)

A short neck denotes a good mind. The messages go quicker to the brain because they don't have as far to go. (**Muriel Spark**)

Minds are like parachutes. They only function when open. (**Lord Dewar**)

Some folks are wise, and some are otherwise. (**Tobias Smollett**)

I am a brain, Watson. The rest of me is a mere appendix. (**Sir Arthur Conan Doyle**)

A thousand Scottish people were asked if they spoke Gaelic. 92% said no, 4% said yes, and 4% said they didn't know. (**Tom Shields**)

F.E. Smith is very clever but sometimes his brains go to his head. (**Margot Asquith**)

The girl who won *Celebrity Big Brother* this year wasn't a celebrity. She didn't know what a gynaecologist was. She thought Hitler could still be alive, and that Dundee was in Wales. (**George Galloway on Chantell Houghton, the 2006 winner**)

Big audiences in Britain are mind dead. The best one I ever played to was in Broadmoor asylum. (**Brian Cox**)

THE LAW

A lawyer is a learned gentleman who rescues your estate from your enemies and keeps it for himself. (**Lord Brougham**)

The law doesn't content itself with classifying and punishing crime. It invents it. (**Norman Douglas**)

Lawyers are the only people in whom ignorance of the law is not punished. (**Lord Brougham**)

According to an old Memphis by-law, a female must not drive an automobile unless she's preceded by a man waving a red flag. (**Richard Wilson**)

I've been involved in so many law cases I've put lawyers' kids through school. (**Sean Connery**)

It's the law that makes the crime. (**A.S. Neill**)

To succeed as a lawyer, you have to have a forensic brain and a desire for a BMW. (**Brian McCardie**)

The Scottish verdict 'Not proven' means 'Guilty, but don't do it again.' (**Winifred Duke**)

LIFE

Everyone sees life through their job. To the doctor, the world is a hospital. To the broker it's a stock exchange, to the lawyer a vast criminal court, to the soldier a barracks and area of manoeuvre, to the farmer soil and bad weather, to truck-drivers a road system, to prostitutes a brothel, to mothers an inescapable nursery, to children a school, to film stars a looking-glass, to undertakers a morgue, and to myself a security installation powered by the sun and only crackable by death. (**Alasdair Gray**)

You're brought up to believe that if you're smart enough and read enough books, you'll find the meaning in things, but part of getting on with life is realising that perhaps there isn't any meaning. (**Robbie Coltrane**)

LITERATURE

At the moment of writing the author is fictive. Only the story is real. (**Tom Docherty**)

If King Lear had been given electric shock treatment, there would have been no need for all that nonsense on the heath. (**R.D. Laing**)

Authors and uncaptured prisoners are the only people in the world who are free from routine. (**Eric Linklater**)

Barabbas was a publisher. (**Thomas Campbell**)

He could as easily have created the planets as written Hamlet. (**Thomas Carlyle on Francis Bacon**)

Biography is one of the new terrors of death. (**John Arbuthnot**)

I own *Harry Potter* so I can do whatever I like to him, even torture him if I wish. (**J.K. Rowling**)

Biographies ought to be written by acute enemies of the subject. (**A.J. Balfour**)

Many friends I've made in journalism over the years have all subscribed to the theory that it might not be the best career to choose if you want a long life. (**Bill McLaren**)

J.K. Rowling's imagination was so amazing that I wanted to crawl into her head. Now that I'm in one of her films, of course, I want to crawl into her bank balance. (**Richard Harris**)

Book promotion tours mean being put up in a five-star hotel, going to a bookshop, drinking sour wine, talking to people who don't want to talk to you, going back to your hotel room with a club sandwich and watching a documentary on East Timor. (**A.L. Kennedy**)

It occurred to me that I would like to be a poet. The chief qualification, I understand, is that you must be born. Well I hunted up my birth certificate and found I was all right on that score. (**Saki**)

A friend once borrowed my early poems. When he gave them back he asked, 'When are you publishing the answers?' (**Norman MacCaig**)

When I hear the words 'Arts Council', I reach for my pistol. (**Ian Hamilton Finlay**)

Incessant scribbling is death to thought. (**Thomas Carlyle**)

Poetry happens between the ears and behind the left nipple. (**Douglas Dunn**)

I'm not too keen on characters taking over a book. They should do as they're darn well told. (**Iain Banks**)

As civilisation advances, poetry almost necessarily declines. (**Lord Macaulay**)

When words depreciate, our awarenesses [sic] go with them. Intensity dilutes and a gantry of potent spirits in replaced by the insipid afternoon tea of complacency. (**William McIlvanney**)

LIVERPOOL FOOTBALL

Kenny Dalglish was quiet in the Liverpool team talks until the players started talking about conditions. Then he came on like a Govan shipyard shop steward. (**Graeme Souness**)

Punter: '£50 on Liverpool to beat Dundee.'
Bookie: 'Sorry, we don't take bets on friendlies.'
Punter: 'Don't be daft – Liverpool don't play friendlies!'
(**Edward Phillips**)

Klopp has re-invigorated the Kop. (**Alex Ferguson**)

LOVE

It is very rarely that a man loves. When he does, it is nearly always fatal. (**Hugh McDiarmid**)

Love has been defined as 'The cognitive-affective state characterised by intrusive and obsessive fantasising concerning reciprocity and amorant feeling by the object of amorance'. But I'm sure it also has some good points. (**Richard Wilson**)

Love makes the world go round, but not as fast as whisky. (**Compton Mackenzie**)

To love another is to see oneself as another to the other. (**R.D. Laing**)

Let no one who loves be called altogether unhappy. Even love unreturned has its rainbow. (**J.M. Barrie**)

I counted my Valentine cards yesterday. It didn't take long as I had exactly none. (**Rhona Cameron**)

Follow love and it will flee. Flee it, and it follows ye. (**Proverb**)

Love and hate are not opposites. The opposite of love is indifference. (**A.S. Neill**)

When Angela told me she loved me I knew in my heart it was my dog she was after. (**Jimmy Logan**)

If Muhammad Ali was a woman I would be in danger of falling in love with him. (**Bill Shankly**)

MARRIAGE

Marriage is a wonderful invention but then again so is the bicycle repair kit. (**Billy Connolly**)

How do most Scotsmen define marriage? As a very expensive way to get their washing done. (**Allan Morrison**)

A husband, returning home in a terrible state at 4 a.m., so infuriated his wife that she threw the alarm clock at him. As his colleagues remarked the next day, 'It's amazing how time flies when you're enjoying yourself.' (**Tom Shields**)

Marriage is a ghastly public confession of a strictly private intention. (**Ian Hay**)

Some people are obsessed with the whole idea of marriage. A woman named Adrienne Cuyot from France was engaged 652 times and married 53 times over a period of 23 years. (**Richard Wilson**)

There's a group for men in Hollywood called Divorce Anonymous. It works like this. If a member of the group starts to feel the urge to divorce, they send over an accountant to talk him out of it. (**Sean Connery**)

There's a sign in the kitchen of our house which states, 'We interrupt this marriage to bring you the football season'. (**Gordon Strachan**)

Being married to Sean Connery was like being married to a golf course. (**Diane Cilento**)

The only difference between the married and the dead is that the married get to watch *Stars in Their Eyes* from a slouching position whereas the dead are contractually obliged to be horizontal. (**Ian Pattison**)

Marriage licences should be renewed annually like dog licences. (**Rod Stewart**)

Christians are only allowed one wife. This is called monotony. (**John G. Muir**)

It was a mixed wedding. She was from Glasgow and he was from Edinburgh. (**Stanley Baxter**)

If I married again I'd be a bigayinamist. (**Billy Connolly**)

The weddings I like best are the ones where I'm not getting married. (**Jimmy Logan**)

The happiest time in anyone's life is just after the first divorce. (**J.K. Galbraith**)

Instead of getting married again I'm going to find a woman I don't like and just give her my house. (**Rod Stewart**)

When Liz Taylor married Larry Fortensky he was younger than her first wedding dress. (**A.A. Gill**)

Show me a good loser and I'll show you a loser. (**Laurie McMenemy**)

Whoever burns his backside must sit on it. (**Proverb**)

Even a broken clock is right twice a day. (**David Steel**)

A change is as good as arrest. (**Bob Cameron**)

It is the mark of a good action that it appears inevitable in retrospect. (**Robert Louis Stevenson**)

History is just a distillation of rumour. (**Thomas Carlyle**)

Art is not a mirror but a hammer. (**John Grierson**)

Even sharks need parasites. (**Ian Pattison**)

The more you know, the less you better. (**Proverb**)

Ideals are like items you pack in your luggage and take with you everywhere but never get to wear. (**William McIlvanney**)

Rudyard Kipling said it's the taking part that counts, not the winning. Well that's a load of shite. (**Andy Goram**)

Stop the world, Scotland wants to get on. (**Winnie Ewing**)

Tragedy can be so quiet and casual and ordinary that sometimes it is gone before we know that it has been. (**William McIlvanney**)

Nothing is so useless as a general maxim. (**Lord Macaulay**)

A little earning is a dangerous thing. (**Bill Nighy**)

Only dead fish swim with the stream. (**Gordon Dunn**)

Life without industry is guilt. Industry without art is brutality. (**John Ruskin**)

Only the mediocre are always at their best. (**Chic Murray**)

Success is backbone, not wishbone. (**Ernest Bromfield**)

The breath of a butterfly's wing in the rain forest is the birth of a tornado in the desert. (**John Fraser**)

History is littered with dead opinion polls. (**Andrew Lang**)

The best way to get the better of temptation is to yield to it. (**Clementina Graham**)

There is so much good in the worst of us, and so much bad in the best of us, it behoves all of us not to talk about the rest of us. (**Robert Louis Stevenson**)

Laugh and the world laughs with you. Quarrel with your wife and you sleep alone. (**Lex McLean**)

We hear war called murder. It is not. It is suicide. (**Ramsay MacDonald**)

There's no greater enemy of art than the pram in the hallway. (**Johnny McBrier**)

Holidays should last long enough for your boss to miss you, but not long enough for him to discover that he can do without you. (**Robert Lang**)

Ask yourself whether you are happy and you cease to be so. (**John Stuart Mill**)

Keeping a secret, to most of us, means only telling a few people. (**Ian Pattison**)

MEANNESS

The vice of meanness, condemned in every other country, is in Scotland translated into a virtue called 'thrift'. (**David Thompson**)

What would you get if you crossed an Irishman with a Scot? An alcoholic who buys drinks wholesale. (**Graffiti**)

The definition of optimism is a Jew who makes a purchase from another Jew and hopes to sell it on to a Scotsman at a profit. (**Tom Shields**)

There was a letter in *The Times* this week from an enraged Aberdonian. 'If you print any more jokes about Scotsmen,' it said, 'I will have to stop borrowing your paper.' (**Fred Metcalf**)

No McTavish/Was ever lavish. (**Ogden Nash**)

You couldn't imagine a bunch of Scotsmen forming the Mafia. It wouldn't occur to them to kill a man and put a fish in his mouth. They'd be like, 'That's a perfectly good herring, Alastair!' (**Robbie Coltrane**)

When Glasgow was made the Cultural Capital of Europe, the inhabitants' reaction was very healthy. They became terrified that it would put 20p on the price of a pint of bitter. (**Jeffrey Bernard**)

A Highlander had just buried his wife and visited the local newspaper to put a notice in the Deaths column. He chose the words 'Muriel's dead'. Upon being informed that he could use more words without incurring any extra cost, he said, 'Och, why don't you add, 'And second-hand tractor for sale'?' (**Frank Carson**)

I once knew a Scotsman who was so mean he only breathed in. (**Bob Monkhouse**)

There was once a Glasgow family who lost a loved one in a fire. He said to the mortuary attendant, 'We want, hauf price at the cremmy!' (**Michael Munro**)

Scotsmen who believe in reincarnation leave everything to themselves. (**Les Dawson**)

A Scottish captain once lent the referee a coin for the toss and demanded his whistle as security. (**Edward Phillips**)

Then there was the Glaswegian who gave his son an empty box for Christmas. He told him it was an Action Man deserter. (**Jim Davidson**)

A Scotsman died of a heart attack throwing a penny to some carol singers. The string broke. (**Colin Crampton**)

There's a sign outside a Scottish cinema that says, 'Free admission for old age pensioners if accompanied by both parents.' (**Bob Monkhouse**)

A Scotsman is someone who, before sending his pyjamas to the laundry, stuffs a sock in each pocket. (**Ambrose Bierce**)

Did you hear about the Scot who took a taxi to the bankruptcy court? When he arrived, he asked the driver in as one of his creditors. (**Penelope Frith**)

And then there was the Scotsman who built himself a round house because he was so afraid of losing a penny in the corner. (**Chubby Brown**)

The following advertisement appeared in a Scottish newspaper: 'A gentleman who has lost a left leg would like to correspond with another who has lost his right one and takes a size nine shoe'. (**Des MacHale**)

Don't believe all that stuff about the Scots being mean – except for one lady I stayed with in Inverness who had a coffee vending machine in the lounge. (**Bill Shipton**)

MISCONCEPTIONS

There's nothing quite like a solemn oath: people always think you mean it. (**Norman Douglas**)

I am not at all the sort of person you and I took me for. (**Jane Welsh Carlyle to her husband in a letter**)

Contrary to belief, I didn't take my wife to see a Rochdale match as an anniversary present. It was her birthday. Would I have got married during the football season? Absolutely not. Anyway it wasn't Rochdale – it was Rochdale Reserves. (**Bill Shankly**)

I was once reported dead in South Africa. A friend of mine believed it and rang my wife. 'I hear that Sean died,' he said. My wife replied, 'I don't think so. He's out playing golf.' (**Sean Connery**)

I always look skint. When I buy a *Big Issue*, people take it out of my hand and give me a pound. (**Billy Connolly**)

I was often accused of copying Bob Dylan because we dressed and sang alike. What was really going on was that we were both copying Woody Guthrie. (**Donovan**)

MIXED METAPHORS

All that was missing was a wee rub of the green. When we went 2–nil down it was like shutting the gate after the horse had bolted. We left ourselves a mountain to climb. (**Dunfermline boss Bert Paton after a defeat**)

For some time now the Italian Government have been tightening the screws on terrorists from both sides of the political rainbow. (**Alexander McLeod**)

Celtic have taken this game by the scruff of the throat. (**John Greig**)

Manchester United have got the bull between their horns now. (**Billy McNeill**)

We can only come out of this game with egg on our faces so it's a real banana skin. (**Ray Stewart**)

At the end of the day it's not the end of the world. (**Jim McLean on Dundee United's defeat in the UEFA Cup in 1987**)

If we get promotion, let's sit down and see where we stand. (**Roy McFarland**)

MONEY

Kenny Dalglish calls all his goals tap-ins until we come to the end of the season and we're talking money. (**Bob Paisley**)

I'm not entirely used to having money. I still go around the house putting out all the unused lights. (**Sean Connery**)

He was so mean it hurt him to go to the bathroom. (**Britt Ekland on Rod Stewart**)

Half a million for Remi Moses? You could have got the original Moses for that. And the tablets as well. (**Tommy Docherty**)

What people who accuse me of selling out for Persil don't realise is that I turn down half a million quid's worth of advertising a year. And it's not the usual sexist crap you see in commercials. It shows a guy doing the washing up while the woman sits on her arse. (**Robbie Coltrane**)

They offered me a handshake of £10,000 to settle amicably. I told them they would have to be a lot more amicable than that. (**Tommy Docherty after being released from Preston Football Club in 1981**)

All respectable people live beyond their incomes nowadays. Those who aren't respectable live beyond other people's. (**Saki**)

The only writing I was ever paid for was a rhyme I did to promote Sunlight soap. (**William MacGonagall**)

Pop music is about stealing pocket money from children. (**Ian Anderson**)

A Scot died and left his cousin all the money his cousin owed him. (**Frank Muir**)

We were so poor my brother was made in Hong Kong. (**Ronnie Corbett**)

Did you hear what happened to Andy McTavish last Saturday? He walked all the way to Wembley for the Cup Final to save on the train fare and then had to pay £20 to get in because he was too tired to climb over the wall. (**Edward Phillips**)

Father's Day always worries me. I'm afraid I'll get something I can't afford. (**Billy Connolly**)

Money doesn't buy you happiness, just a miserable form of comfort. (**Lorraine Kelly**)

The Scottish National Gallery of Modern Art paid £3000 in 1982 for a work by sculptor Cesor Baldachini: a six-foot block of rusting car parts crushed into shape by a hydraulic press. The gallery felt the sculpture would help people understand 20th century artistic thinking. A local scrap merchant seemed to agree. He immediately offered to create the same effect for £6. (**Philip Mason**)

I appeared at Carnegie Hall one night with Bob Dylan. I got $200 and he got $60. I told him it would be a year before he cracked Britain. (**Matt McGinn**)

He's so small we didn't have to pay VAT on his playing kit. (**George Fulston on the diminutive Jamie Patterson, who signed for Falkirk in 1994**)

Jock was delirious with excitement when he won the Lottery. 'What about the begging letters?' his wife enquired.
'Just keep sending them,' he advised. (**Brian Johnston**)

Before I became rich I remember reaching the supermarket check-out counting out my money in coppers, finding out I

was two pence short for a tin of baked beans and feeling I had
to pretend I had mislaid a £10 note for the benefit of the bored
girl at the till. (**J. K. Rowling**)

MUSIC

I expect to be making music until I lose my hands and my ears and my heart stops beating. I might be able to do without my hands, but definitely not my ears. (**Alex Kapranos**)

Bands are the only kinds of musical groups in the world that sound better out of tune. I like them when they're good and love them when they're bad. (**Billy Connolly**)

The reason some people don't like your music is the same reason other people do. (**Kirsty McColl**)

The best place to listen to bagpipes being played in Scotland is London. (**Archie McLeod**)

How do you know when you've tuned the bagpipes? (**Tommy Gemmill**)

How can you tell if there's a banjo player at the door? He can't find the key and he doesn't know when to come in. (**Tom Shields**)

I once saw an ad in the *Glasgow Herald* that went, 'Bagpipes for sale. Used only once owing to a bereavement.' (**Billy Connolly**)

Playing the bagpipes for the first time is like having sex with an octopus. (**Andrew McDonald**)

Song writing is like psychic wrestling. (**Annie Lennox**)

Music is everybody's mother. (**Donovan**)

Twelve highlanders and a bagpipe make a rebellion. (**Sir Walter Scott**)

My earliest public performance was in aid of the war effort. It was in a concert for the Spitfire Fund, for which I think I raised about £9. I wore a dressing gown and carried a candle and sang a Christopher Robin song, while standing on the flat roof of an air raid shelter in the communal garden behind our tenement. I like to think I helped undermine German morale. (**Ronnie Corbett**)

The Irish gave the bagpipes to the Scots as a joke but the Scots haven't got it yet. (**Oliver Herford**)

I can't believe that out of 100,000 sperm, you were the quickest one. (**Sheena Easton to a heckler**)

The eighties was a strange time for music. You went from Sid Vicious wanting to kick your bollocks to Boy George wanting to kiss them. (**Ally McCoist**)

What's the difference between Walt Disney and Frank Sinatra? One sings, and the other disnae! (**Tommy McTaig**)

People sometimes say to me that it can't be much fun playing an instrument when I'm deaf but it is. Sometimes I hug loudspeakers between my knees to get the feel of the music. In fact I once gave a performance in Brussels where the deaf people in the audience were put sitting on wooden benches so they could feel the vibrations through the floor. They were also given balloons to hold on to for the same effect. (**Evelyn Glennie**)

I'd rather sweep the stage than resort to the job I was destined to take when I left school. (**Jackie Dennis**)

Beethoven always sounds like the upsetting of bags, with here and there a dropped hammer. (**John Ruskin**)

A record I made was in the shops so long, the hole in the middle healed up. (**Andy Cameron**)

A British company is developing computer chips that store and play music in female breast implants. This is being hailed as a major breakthrough since women are always complaining about men staring at their breasts and not listening to them. (**Pat Roller**)

The Bay City Rollers were once arrested in Africa for overdue bills. They forgot to pay the audience. (**Andy Hamilton**)

He was the eternal optimist. In 1968 he believed Glenn Miller was still just missing. (**Paddy Crerand on Sir Matt Busby. Miller's plane disappeared on a flight from England to France in 1944**)

The bagpipes sound the same when you've finished learning them as when you start. (**Sir Thomas Beecham**)

What would you call 2,000 banjos thrown into the river Clyde? A good start. (**Tom Shields**)

The main musical instrument in my house was the radio. (**Midge Ure**)

I don't think he was ever born to be a rock 'n' roll star. He was probably born to be chairman of Watford Football Club. And now he's beginning to look like the chairman of Watford Football Club as well. (**Rod Stewart on Elton John in 1977**)

I'm capable of being a rock 'n' roll star and the chairman of Watford Football Club, and I sell more records than Rod

Stewart. Anyway, he should stick to grave-digging, 'cos that's where he belongs, six feet under. (**Elton John in reply**)

The reason bagpipers walk when they play is to get away from the noise. (**Spike Milligan**)

NAMES

Fumes in a hold had overcome Archie. As he was being carried into the ambulance, the driver said, 'Gie's yer name so we can tell yer family'. 'But ma family already know ma name,' came the reply. (**Allan Morrison**)

How many Scottish Liberal Democrat MPs does it take to change a lightbulb? None. They're too busy changing the party name. (**Tom Shields**)

My real name is Jim. Midge is that spelt backwards – sort of. (**Midge Ure**)

Elton John decided he wanted to re-name Watford. He wanted to call it Queen of the South. (**Tommy Docherty**)

Bonnie Prince Charlie was the only man ever to be named after three sheepdogs. (**John Ross**)

The last player to score a hat trick in the F.A. Cup Final was Stan Mortenson. He even had a final named after him, the Matthews Final. (**Laurie McMenemy**)

Ma name is Lucifer. Ma mither gied it me. She tocht it had a ring tae it. (**James Robertson**)

When *Dr No* went to Japan, they translated it as *No Need For Any Doctors*. (**Sean Connery**)

She should have been called Marie Stops. (**Duncan Murray on birth control pioneer Marie Stopes**)

They've nicknamed me Ena Sharples because my head was never out of the net. (**Goalkeeper Ian Thain after letting in ten against Rangers in 1996**)

Oban boasts a lawyer by the name of Robin Banks. (**Tom Shields**)

There was a composer once who took a manuscript round Tin Pan Alley. All the publishers agreed it was the most beautiful music they ever heard, but he refused to let them publish it because they wouldn't agree to him calling it 'I Love You So Much, You Make Me Want the Lavatory'. (**Matt McGinn**)

NONSENSE

It is not contrary to reason to prefer the destruction of the whole world to the scratching of my finger. (**David Hume**)

I can talk on any subject as long as it's football. (**Tommy Docherty**)

The U.S. economy doesn't need fiscal rectitude. It needs rectal fiscitude. (**Billy Connolly**)

We murdered them nil–all. (**Bill Shankly**)

I can drink like a chimney. (**Alex Ferguson**)

Our house is so big at the moment, I had to call Penn on my mobile the other day to find out what room she was in. (**Rod Stewart on the pressures of life with Penny Lancaster**)

In 1983, magistrates rejected an application for a sports and social club because the building was deemed to be a fire hazard. The applicants were… the local fire brigade. (**Richard Wilson**)

I once spotted a sign in America that said: 'To The Braille School'. (**Billy Connolly**)

You're the spitting image of yourself. (**A fan to Ewan McGregor**)

In the army, 'crime' may range from being unshaven on parade to irrevocably perforating your rival in love with a bayonet. (**Ian Hay**)

Our nose is badly designed: the snot falls out. It should really be the other way round. But then when you sneezed, your hair would get two side partings and your eyes would be full of snot. Also, you'd drown when it rained. Isn't life complex? (**Billy Connolly**)

Scottish artist William Turnbull won second prize of £3,000 for his blank canvas painted white at the John Moore art exhibition in Liverpool in 1978. Called 'Untitled No. 9', it could be hung either way. 'The back of the picture has 'Top' written on both its top and bottom,' Turnbull said, 'because basically both experiences are correct. It is not gravitationally oriented.' (**Philip Mason**)

Security at Anfield is a bit over the top. Kenny Dalglish told me once he wasn't allowed in because he didn't have a pass. Kenny Dalglish! (**Andy Gray**)

The Gallowgate district where I was born was full of stories, like Joe the Bull saying to a man, 'Was it you or your brother that had the fatal accident?' (**Matt McGinn**)

Notice outside a Clyde shipyard: 'Today's launch has been called off due to flooding.' (**Allan Morrison**)

It will be a shame if either side lose. And that applies to both sides. (**Jock Brown**)

The only time they seem to get the ball is when they give it away. (**Ian St. John**)

One day the headmaster came into the room, looked at the day's numbers and said, 'Thirty-six present in the morning, only thirty-five in the afternoon. Stand up the one who's absent.' (**John Muir**)

The one thing I didn't expect is the way we didn't play. (**George Graham**)

The king told me he would never have died if it had not been for that fool Dawson of Penn. (**Margot Asquith**)

Scotland doesn't have to score tonight, but they do have to win. (**Billy McNeill**)

Four single £1 notes lost on January 27th, vicinity Market St. Sentimental value. Reward. (**Advertisement in Aberdeen newspaper**)

Did you hear about the Scottish kamikaze pilot? He crashed his plane in his brother's scrapyard. (**Jim Davidson**)

OBSERVATIONS AND OPINIONS

If you analyse a glass of water you're left with a lot of chemical components but nothing you can drink. (**J.B.S. Haldane**)

My father told me that if you saw a man in a Rolls Royce, you could be sure he wasn't a gentleman unless he was the chauffeur. (**Lord Arran**)

I hate people who say 'Can I ask you a question?' They don't really give you a choice. (**Billy Connolly**)

Sometimes there's nothing better to do in life than just tidying out your knicker drawer while humming along to Radio 2. (**Lorraine Kelly**).

Clear soup is a more important element of life than a clear conscience. (**Saki**)

The quickest way to make a red light turn green is to try and find something in the glove compartment. (**Billy Connolly**)

Guilt isn't an emotion in the Celtic countries. It's a way of life. (**A.L. Kennedy**)

There's nothing so unnatural as the commonplace. (**Sir Arthur Conan Doyle**)

The most beautiful red rose in the world is a weed if it finds itself flourishing in a cultivated cabbage patch. (**Matt McGinn**)

PARENTHOOD

From the moment of birth, when the Stone Age baby confronts the 20th century mother, the baby is subjected to forces of violence called love as its mother and father, and their parents before them, have been. The initial act of brutality is the mother's first kiss. (**R.D. Laing**)

I want to have a baby and I want Peter Jennings to be the father. I know he's married but we could just have a cheap and tawdry affair. (**Sheena Easton**)

My father had two families. The other one was Manchester United. (**Sandy Busby, Sir Matt's son**)

Most children are reared on a tissue of lies and ignorant prohibitions. (**A.S. Neill**)

When McTaggart ran away from home, his parents rented out the room. (**James Orr**)

Anyone who sleeps like a baby obviously doesn't have one. (**Sybil McCaig**)

Parents attach far too much importance to tidiness. It is one of the seven deadly virtues. (**A.S. Neill**)

Nobody can misunderstand a boy like his mother. (**Norman Douglas**)

No man is responsible for his father. That is entirely his mother's affair. (**Margaret Turnbull**)

As a parent I do everything except breastfeeding. (**Andy Gray**)

I wouldn't mind being remembered as a good parent but we won't know whether I've achieved that until my daughter writes *J.K. Dearest*. (**J.K. Rowling**)

Their eldest son was a disappointment to them. They wanted him to be a linguist and he ended up becoming a Trappist monk. (**Saki**)

I thought she wanted an autograph but instead she said, 'I think I'm your mother'. There's no answer to that, so I bought her a drink. (**Billy Connolly on meeting his mother, who'd deserted him in childhood**)

PEOPLE AND PLACES

New York had the biggest, shiniest apples I'd ever seen, and strawberries the size of oranges. (**Lulu**)

London – that monstrous tuberosity of civilised life. (**Thomas Carlyle**)

Wales must be the only country in the world where one regularly hears nationalists denouncing nationalism. (**Tom Nairn**)

That great cesspool into which all the loungers of Europe are irresistibly drained. (**Sir Arthur Conan Doyle on London**)

When a boy is bored with Glasgow he is ready to live. (**Ian Pattison**)

His mother lived at Bethnal Green, which was not altogether his fault. (**Saki**)

Helensburgh is a wonderfully exciting place, full of entertainment. I weighed myself twice when I was there. (**Chic Murray**)

When you were brought up in working-class Lanarkshire in the 1960s and 70s you got to know your lot in life very quickly. Those who broke the rules were dealt with harshly but if you became a success everyone would claim to know you or your wee sister or your second cousin who played accordion in an orange band in New Stevenson in 1967. (**Elaine C. Smith**)

Oban would be fine if it weren't for all the people. (**Annie Swan**)

There are only two classes of person in New South Wales: those who've been convicted and those who ought to have been. (**Lachlan MacQuarle**)

Canada is all right really, but not for the whole weekend. (**Saki**)

A friend of mine bought a castle in Scotland. When his daughter had a birthday party, he hired a bouncy council estate. (**Harry Hill**)

If we destroy Kansas, the world may not hear about it for years. (**Sean Connery**)

London, oh dull and witless city. Very hell for the restless, inquiring, sensitive soul. Paradise for the snob, the parasite, the prig, the pimp, the placeman and the cheapjack. (**James Bridie**)

Oban has become the Blackpool of the southern Highlands. (**Tom Morton**)

I live in Glasgow because that's where my record collection is. (**Alex Kapranos**)

Edinburgh is the loft extension of England. (**Al Murray**)

'Honolulu' is when you give an MBE to a Scottish singer. (**Barry Cryer**)

There was lots of rain on the Isle of Skye. I asked a man for directions to Dunvegan Castle. He said it was ten miles as the crow floats. (**Les Dawson**)

You had to sleep with your socks on in Burnbank if you wanted them in the morning. Pit-bull terriers had to run about in pairs up there. (**Walter McGowan**)

Dunoon has all the atmosphere of the inside of a wardrobe. (**Rab C. Nesbitt**)

London is a splendid place to live – for those who cannot get out of it. (**Arthur Balfour**)

When I was at St. Mirren's it was a desolate place. Even the birds woke up coughing. (**Alex Ferguson**)

I once spent a week in Greenock one night. (**Lachlan Blair**)

England – the world's busybody. (**Thomas Carlyle**)

The Great Wall of China, I've been told, is the only man-made structure on earth that is visible from the moon. For the life of me I cannot see why anyone would go to the moon to look at it when, with much less difficulty, it can be viewed from China. (**J.K. Galbraith**)

Hillhead used to be so rough you had to put your name down to get mugged. It's so rough there they've got Tom Conti as the Avon Lady. There were so many fiddles going on, Mantovani could have been the District Clerk. (**Chic Murray**)

The Scot perceives a colossal fuss being made about nothing, whereas the Welsh nationalist is intrigued by a country where there seems nothing to make a fuss about. (**Tom Nairn**)

I came to Ireland for a fortnight and stayed six years. (**Mike Scott of The Waterboys**)

I don't know what effect the Edinburgh Military Tattoo has upon the enemy, but – by God – it terrifies me. (**Anthony Troon**)

There was so much to see in Aberdeen I can't begin to list it all. The highlight was a small tot sitting in the doorway of an estate house attempting to smash a 9-volt battery with an axe. (**Rich Hall**)

Edinburgh – a dignified spinster with syphilis. (**Charles Higham**)

POLITICS

Most Scots would be able to identify six vegetables but only two MSPs. (**Rory Bremner**)

Our establishment has presided over economic decline and bequeathed a culture of mediocrity. Why join a bunch of losers? (**Andrew Neil**)

Politics is perhaps the only profession for which no preparation is thought necessary. (**Robert Louis Stevenson**)

Voting Tory is like being in trouble with the police. You'd rather the neighbours didn't know. (**Charles Kennedy**)

For some time, Scotland's greatest exports to England have included whisky and Scottish MPs. Or, in the case of Charles Kennedy, both. (**Rory Bremner**)

Once the king of the jungle, now just the fireside rug. (**Gordon Brown on Michael Heseltine in 1992**)

There's a hell of a lot of politics in football. I don't think Henry Kissinger would have lasted 48 hours at Old Trafford. (**Tommy Docherty**)

David Steel always reminds me of his Spitting Image puppet: desperately trying to bite off someone he'll never be able to chew. (**Jean Rook**)

How many Scottish politicians does it take to change a light bulb? None. Scottish politicians don't change anything. (**Norman McBrier**)

Ramsay MacDonald has, more than any other man, the gift of compressing the largest number of words into the smallest amount of thought. (**Winston Churchill**)

Ministers aren't puppets on strings today. They're the fifth little herring on the end of the rod. (**Nicholas Fairbairn**)

There was no retirement, no concealment. He died by inches in public, the sole mourner at his own protracted funeral. (**Lord Rosebery on Randolph Churchill**)

I have only three words to say about Scottish Nationalism – and two of them are 'Scottish Nationalism.' (**Billy Connolly**)

To listen to some people in politics, you'd think that 'nice' was a 4-lettered word. (**David Steel**)

Trickle-down theory perpetrates the less than elegant metaphor that if one feeds the horse enough oats, some will pass through to the road for the sparrows. (**D.K. Galbraith**)

Henry Campbell-Bannerman has all the qualifications for a great Literal Prime Minister. He wears spats and he has a beautiful set of false teeth. (**R.B. Graham**)

David Lloyd George couldn't see a belt without hitting below it. (**Margot Asquith**)

The English politician's view of Scotland is of an old pot seething with dissatisfaction which fortunately can be relied on never to come to the boil. (**Edwin Morgan**)

The main difference between devolution and evolution is that devolution takes longer. (**Ewen Bain**)

I would rather consult my valet than the Conservative conference. (**Arthur Balfour**)

There's a story that when Margaret Thatcher first met Gorbachev, he gave her a ball-point pen and she offered him Scotland. (**Nicholas Shakespeare**)

The desire to become a politician should, by definition, prohibit one from doing so. (**Arnold Baillie**)

Sometimes in politics you just have to lie. I think we should be truthful about that. (**Charles Kennedy**)

The Reformation was a kind of spiritual strychnine of which Scotland took an overdose. (**Willa Muir**)

The Honorary Lady should remember that she was an egg once. Many members of the House may regret that it was ever fertilised. (**Nicholas Fairbairn on Edwina Currie**)

If David Cameron hadn't gone to Eton he'd be managing a Pizza Hut now. (**Frankie Boyle**)

Politics is show business for ugly people. (**George Galloway**)

I don't go to the House of Lords anymore. The last time I was there a bishop stole my umbrella. (**Lord Berners**)

My wife is a Scottish Nationalist and a Socialist. Can you imagine a more ridiculous combination? (**Alasdair Gray**)

Ever since *Big Brother,* a vote for George Galloway is a vote for feline erotica. (**Russell Brand**)

Most politicians look like people who have become human by correspondence course. (**A.A. Gill**)

Paddy Ashdown is the only party leader to be a trained killer. Mrs Thatcher was self-taught. (**Charles Kennedy**)

The first time I took my seat in Westminster it was said by political pundits that a chill ran along the Labour benches looking for a spine to run up. (**Winnie Ewing**)

PRAISE

The three greatest football managers of all time were Jock Stein, Jock Stein and Jock Stein. (**Doug McLeod**)

It was worth missing a train – and sometimes you had to do that – while he rummaged for the right word. (**J.M. Barrie on Henry James**)

Once again it was Gough who stood firm for Scotland in the air. (**Jock Brown**)

George Best's balance was so good he disproved the law of gravity. If Isaac Newton ever saw him play he would have just eaten the apple. (**Hugh McIlvanney**)

PREDICTIONS

If Jesus were to come back today, people wouldn't even crucify him. They would ask him to dinner, listen to what he had to say, and then make fun of it. (**Thomas Carlyle**)

This is my prediction for the future. Whatever hasn't happened will happen. (**J.B.S. Haldane**)

When I started out at nineteen I made myself three promises: to stay in a job for more than six months, to save £300 to buy a sports car, and to pull as many birds as I could. All those dreams have come wonderfully true. (**Rod Stewart**)

A friend of mine once predicted that by 1984 postmen would be armed and carry tear gas and would make their deliveries by Panzer tank. As we now know, he was totally wrong in his judgment – except for certain parts of Paisley. (**Ian Pattison**)

PRIVACY

When I was in Japan filming You Only Live Twice, the paparazzi appeared in the toilet. They had their cameras coming in under the door. (**Sean Connery**)

The appeal of being alone is not the absence of others, it's the presence of me. When I'm with other people, I can't find me. I become the spectre at the feast. (**Billy Connolly**)

To a child, the toilet is the most interesting room in any house. (**A.S. Neill**)

You have to know a man awfully well in Canada to know his surname. (**John Buchan**)

PUNS

I'm drinking from a cup today. I'd prefer a mug, but they're all in the boardroom. (**Tommy Docherty**)

I knew it was going to be a bad day. My karma ran over my dogma. (**Ronnie Corbett**)

Dr Donne's verses are like the peace of God – they pass all understanding. (**King James 1**)

Beauty is only sin deep. (**Saki**)

Eric Cantona couldn't tackle a fish supper. (**Alex Ferguson**)

Throughout my life, radio has been a great turn-on for me. (**Andy Cameron**)

What did Dracula get when he came to Glasgow? A bat in the mouth. (**Michael Munro**)

I walked into the bedroom. The curtains were drawn but the furniture was real. (**Chic Murray**)

The Prime Minister had discussions this morning with the Cabinet. He then spoke to the wardrobe, the sideboard and the chest of drawers. (**Ronnie Corbett**)

I sometimes feel church services should have a five-minute 'coughie' break. (**James Simpson**)

You can drag a horse to water but a pencil must be lead. (**Chic Murray**)

I was standing at the bus stop the other day when a man came up to me and said, 'Have you got a light, mac?' I said, 'No, I've got a dark brown overcoat'. (**Chic Murray**)

RELIGION

It angers me to see Rangers or Celtic fanatics getting all steamed up in the name of religion when most of them have never been near a church in years. (**Derek Johnstone**)

Saints have died out from sheer inability to propagate their species. (**Norman Douglas**)

Oysters are more beautiful than any religion. There's nothing in Christianity or Buddhism that quite matches their sympathetic unselfishness. (**Saki**)

Perhaps God is not dead, but mad. (**R.D. Laing**)

Roman Catholics have shaken off the nightmare of monotheism. Their Trinity is broken up, the Holy Ghost having evaporated in the course of years as spirits often do. (**Norman Douglas**)

Heaven for the climate, hell for the company. (**J.M. Barrie**)

Poor Matthew Arnold, he's gone to heaven, no doubt. But he won't like God. (**Robert Louis Stevenson**)

I only want to go to heaven if Hank Williams is there. (**Billy Connolly**)

I don't suppose angels have any sense of humour. It would be of no use to them anyway because they never hear any jokes. (**Saki**)

The fashion just now is a Roman Catholic frame of mind and an agnostic conscience. You get the medieval picturesqueness of the one with the modern conveniences of the other. (**Saki**)

Nothing in the world delights the truly religious so much as consigning them to eternal damnation. (**James Hogg**)

Tommy Docherty died and went to heaven. God said, 'Who are you?' as he strode up to the celestial throne. 'I'm Tommy Docherty,' he replied, 'and that's my chair you're sitting in.' (**Edward Phillips**)

I have listened to many a windbag full of sermons in my day. I am no revivalist, but of late I have come to dread the milk-and-water flapdoodle of play-safe parsons. (**A.J. Cronin**)

The Scotchman would as soon tell a funny story in a church-yard as in a bar-room. (**Stephen Leacock**)

It wasn't a woman who betrayed Jesus with a kiss. (**Catherine Carswell**)

At the last judgment, the Scots will cry out, faced with hell fire, 'Lord, Lord, we didna ken!', and the Lord will look down and remark affably 'Ay, weel, ye ken noo'! (**Iain Finlayson**)

Two Scotsmen had been rowed across the Sea of Galilee but complained of the high fare. Said one, 'You can cross Loch Lomond for one and ninepence'. The boatman quietly and reverentially replied, 'But this is the sea upon which Our Lord appeared.' At which point a voice from the bow could be heard saying, 'No wonder He walked!' (**Anne Sisson**)

I'm a Catholic atheist rather than a Protestant one. (**Duncan Carlyle**)

My preference is for Scottish Calvinism. Nothing makes us happier than misery. (**James Reston**)

Catholics are travel agents for guilt trips. (**John Ross**)

From the fact that there are four million species of beetles on this planet, but only eight thousand species of mammals, I conclude that the Creator, if He exists, has a special preference for beetles. (**J.B.S. Haldane**)

I went to confession and told the priest I had bad thoughts. 'Do you entertain these thoughts?' he asked me. 'No,' I replied, 'but they sure entertain me!' (**Stanley Baxter**)

The reason Jesus wasn't born in Glasgow is because they couldn't find a virgin or three wise men. (**Tommy Leyton**)

Cricket is a game which the English, not being a spiritual people, have invented in order to give themselves some conception of eternity. (**Lord Mancroft**)

Heading in the Catholic Herald: Catholic MPs swing both ways on hanging vote'. (**Tom Shields**)

Every religion has a birth, a youth, an old age and a death. The idea of God changes as culture changes. A creative God is not wanted in an age that can make its own atom bombs. (**A.S. Neill**)

As a child I experienced the rigours of the Scottish Sabbath. The highlight was a visit to the cemetery. (**T.C. Smout**)

Scottish by birth, British by law, and a highlander by the grace of God. (**Traditional saying**)

A Scot is a man who keeps the Sabbath, and everything else he can lay his hands on. (**Chic Murray**)

In Scotland even Protestants suffer from Catholic guilt. (**Ian Pattison**)

Jock, feeling full of religious fervour and Scotch whisky, hurled a bottle of Domestos through the window of his local church. He was fined for bleach of the priest. (**Des MacHale**)

REPARTEE

Doug Ellis, the Villa chairman, said he was right behind me. I told him I'd sooner have him in front of me where I could see him. (**Tommy Docherty**)

I don't know. It's years since I've been to bed with a sixty year old man. (**Sean Connery after being asked on his sixtieth birthday if he thought sixty year old men were virile**)

When the TV people asked me if I'd like to play a football manager in a play, I asked how long it would take. They told me about ten days. 'That's about par for the course,' I replied. (**Tommy Docherty**)

Four grand? I could buy a new one for that! (**Rod Stewart to a woman who priced an antique he was viewing at £4000**)

Velocity. (**Kenny Dalglish to a reporter who asked him for a 'quick word' after a match**)

I'm sorry to hear that, sir. You don't happen to have it on you now, do you? (**Tommy Sheridan to his father after being told he was going to be cut out of his will with a shilling**).

Here's 20p – phone all of them. (**Gordon Brown to Peter Mandelson after Mandelson asked him for 10p to phone a friend**)

Crossing Piccadilly Circus. (**Joseph Thomson after being asked what was the most dangerous part of a trip he took to Africa**)

How was it for you? (**Angela Ramsay when she was frisked by an airport official once**)

Not yet, laddie, not yet. (**Finlay Curris when asked at the age of ninety if he'd ever played a romantic lead in a movie**)

RETIREMENT

The reason I'm back is because the wife wants me out of the house. (**Kenny Dalglish upon returning to football management in 1991 after a spell away from it**)

When I retired I was inundated with all kinds of testimonials, dinners and calls asking me to do this and that. One day I said to my wife that perhaps I shouldn't have retired after all – it was too much like hard work. (**Bill McLaren**)

My lifeblood is the theatre. I wasn't about to let the small matter of a quadruple bypass operation take that away from me. (**Jimmy Logan upon returning to the stage after life-saving surgery**)

I'm retired. I'm now officially a lower form of animal life than a Duracell battery. I've been replaced by a box. It's standard procedure for a man my age. The next stage is to stick you inside one. (**Richard Wilson on his role as Victor Meldrew**)

THE ROYALTY

Strip your Louis Quatorze of his king-gear and there's nothing left but a poor forked radish with a head fantastically carved. (**Thomas Carlyle on King Louis X1V**)

Mary Queen of Scots brought her dog with her to her execution. Greater love than this no woman hath. (**Richard Wilson**)

He speaks to me as if I were a public meeting. (**Queen Victoria on William Gladstone**)

The wisest fool in Christendom (**King Henry V1 on James 1**)

She'll have to walk behind the angels and she won't like that. (**Edward V11 after being asked if he thought Queen Victoria would be happy in heaven**)

Mary Queen of Scots had the morals of a well-intentioned but hysterical poodle. (**Lewis Grassic Gibbon**)

RUGBY

It's been a bloody awful year for injuries. I've got a steel plate across my cheek, three along the jaw and eight staples in my head. The last time I practised it was raining. I had to pack it in because I was starting to rust. (**Derek White in 1991**)

What you rugby types have managed to do to such a simple object as a ball appals me. Thank goodness you weren't around when the wheel was invented. (**John Rafferty**)

I'm amphibious. I can kick with both feet. (**Brian Hegarty**)

The knee doesn't bother me when I'm walking but it's painful when I kneel – like before the bank manager. (**David Leslie**)

Rugby is the only sport I know where you can put your head up the other player's bum without the ref blowing his whistle. (**Ally McCoist**)

RUTHLESSNESS

If you murder a player he'll be psychologically beaten before he goes on the table the next time you meet. I enjoy doing that. (**Stephen Hendry**)

Should Gheorghe Hagi become just a traction more clinical in slicing open the opposition, he may have to play the rest of the World Cup in a mask and gown. (**Hugh McIlvanney on the 1994 competition**)

A diary is an assassin's cloak which we wear when we stab a comrade in the back with a pen. (**William Soutar**)

Sir Matthew spent the morning designing mausoleums for his enemies. (**Eric Linklater**)

Referees at Celtic-Rangers matches always have a hard time. One particular unfortunate, officiating at his first fixture, was checking in with the team managers before the kick-off. 'Well that seems to be everything,' said the Rangers boss, 'Now if you'd just like to give us the name and address of your next-of-kin, we can start the match.' (**Edward Phillips**)

The best way to deal with Ronaldo is to stop the ball getting to him in the first place. If it does get to him, we have to make sure he has no space to turn. If that doesn't work, we'll have to tie his shoelaces together. (**John Collins on Scotland's forth-coming World Cup tie with Brazil in 1998**)

SARCASM

Gentlemen, I admit Napoleon was a monster, but we must be just to our great enemy. We must not forget that he once shot a bookseller. (**Thomas Campbell**)

It was a Scottish wedding. The confetti was on elastic. (**Fred Metcalf**)

It was very good of God to let Carlyle and Mrs Carlyle marry one another and thereby only make two people miserable instead of four. (**Samuel Butler**)

Don Francesco was a fisher of men and of women. It was his way of taking exercise. (**Norman Douglas**)

Three platoons out of four in our company are at present commanded by NCOs, one of whom has been picked out of the ranks simply because he possesses a loud voice and a cake of soap. (**Ian Hay**)

My second spell at Villa ended in the summer of 1987 with the arrival of Graham Taylor. You could say it resulted from a clash of personalities. I had one and he didn't. (**Andy Gray**)

In the World Darts Championship of 1982, Jocky Wilson missed when attempting to shake hands with an opponent. (**Craig Brown**)

Half of them were booing and half of them were cheering. The only problem was that the half that were cheering were cheering the half that were booing. (**Brown when he was managing Clyde in 1996**)

A Scottish farmer was approached by a former ploughman who said he was on the trail of a job and wondered whether he would give him a character reference. 'Oh I could gie ye that,' said the farmer, 'but I think ye might manage better without it.' (**James Simpson**)

Teacher to pupil: 'This is an axle in my hand. At the end of it is a crank'. Pupil: Which end, sir?' (**John Muir**)

Americans are too clean to revolt. They spend all their time changing their shirts and washing themselves. You can't feel fierce and revolutionary in a bathroom. (**Eric Linklater**)

What really impressed me about America was the plenitude, of all-night walk-in taxidermy stores. How convenient! (**Billy Connolly**)

If all else fails, immortality can always be assured by spectacular error. (**J.K. Galbraith**)

A large poster headed 'Man Wanted For Murder' was placed outside a Glasgow Police station. 200 men applied for the job. (**Stanley Baxter**)

My career was unscathed by Live Aid. I didn't have to play Saint Midge because that burden was spread across Bob Geldof's shoulders. (**Midge Ure**)

David Batty is quite prolific, isn't he? He scores a goal a season, regular as clockwork. (**Kenny Dalglish**)

I agree that passive smoking is outrageous. They should pay for their own. (**Rhona Craigie**)

She looks as if her idea of a good time would be knitting, preferably under the guillotine. (**William McIlvanney**)

Dennis Price's suicide bid did wonders for his career. (**John Fraser**)

Stephen Hendry is the only man I know whose face comes with free garlic bread. (**Nick Hancock**)

'Rosetti, dear Rosetti, I love your work, but you were really a bit of a berk'. (**George MacBeth**)

On a train from Inverness to Glasgow, as it neared its destination and people began to assemble their belongings, a passenger remarked 'Well, that's the worst of the journey over.' 'Where are you going to?' asked his neighbour. 'China,' was the reply. (**David Ross**)

Ramsay MacDonald has the gift of compressing the largest amount of words into the smallest amount of thought. (**Winston Churchill**)

Fifty-seven types of alien life forms have been catalogued, some of which look just like humans. They could walk among us and you wouldn't know the difference. This would certainly explain David Coulthard. (**Jeremy Clarkson**)

One of the best ways to avoid necessary and even urgent tasks is to seem to be busily employed on things that are already done. (**J.K. Galbraith**)

I've been dismissed as a blimpish, right-wing dinosaur. Those of an ultra-liberal persuasion can console themselves with the thought that my kind won't be around much longer. Then they can get on with wrecking civilisation in peace. (**George MacDonald Fraser**)

Lord Rosebery was a man who never missed an opportunity to miss an opportunity. (**George Bernard Shaw**)

Lonnie Donegan was such a nervous man he wore water wings in the shower. (**Chic Murray**)

Oh for an hour of Herod. (**Anthony Hope at the opening of *Peter Pan* in 1904**)

Advertising researchers are blind men groping in a dark room for a black cat that isn't there. (**Ludovic Kennedy**)

I Saw Partick Thistle score. (**Bumper Sticker**)

Peter Swales likes publicity. He wears a card around his neck saying, 'In case of heart attack, call a press conference.' (**Tommy Docherty**)

If editors of upmarket newspapers have a popular thought they have to go into a darkened room and lie down until it passes. (**Kelvin Mackenzie**)

The more I read Socrates, the less I wonder why they poisoned him. (**Lord Macaulay**)

Tim Henman returns serve with the kind of filthy looks he hasn't had cause to throw since his wild teenage years when he threw a strop over not being allowed to watch Pogle's Wood and he had to be sent to bed without any tea. (**Aidan Smith**)

All men are born equal but quite a few get over it. (**Lord Mancroft**)

In his prime Joe Bugner had the physique of a Greek statue, but fewer moves. (**Hugh McIlvanney**)

My two chief ambitions are to pay off my mortgage as soon as possible, and to see Stuart Taylor go to the bar. (**Ian Maxwell**)

SCOTLAND BY SCOTS

Teacher to class: 'What did the Scots call Scotland before the English arrived?' Wee Jimmy stuck up his hand. 'Oors, sir'. (**Allan Morrison**)

The typical Scot has bad teeth, a good chance of cancer, a liver under severe stress and a heart attack pending. He smokes like a chimney, drinks like a fish, and regularly makes an exhibition of himself. Apart from that he's fine. (**Alan Bold**)

Scotland is bounded on the south by England, on the east by the rising sun, on the north by the Arory-bory-Alice, and on the west by eternity. (**Nan Shepherd**)

The most Scottish thing I've ever seen was when I was going through a town called Bathgate at about 11.30 one night and saw a guy pissing against a front door. He then took out his keys and went inside. (**Frankie Boyle**)

Inhabiting a small impoverished country ridged by bleak mountains and ringed by rocky coasts against which rough seas sweep and surge, the Scots are hardy, frugal, thrifty, resolute and addicted to 'usquebaugh', a Gaelic word vilely corrupted by the Saxons to 'whisky'. (**A.J. Cronin**)

Like most Scottish men, my father loved everything that was bad for him. (**Rhona Cameron**)

I don't think we can ever be completely separate from England. It's one big bloody island at the end of the day. (**Sharleen Spiteri**)

Scottish summers consist of three hot days and a thunder-storm. (**John Aiton**)

You know it's summer in Scotland because the rain gets warmer. (**Tommy McFarlane**)

The Scots kept on compulsively sticking their noses in other people's business through the ages, going either where they had no right or where no person in his right senses would have thought of going in the first place. Find a man herding sheep in the furthest reaches of Patagonia and the chances are that he is a Scot. (**Alastair MacLean**)

The Scots have transformed guilt into an art form. (**Arnold Rafferty**)

Scotsmen don't paw girls on dates. They're too busy holding onto their wallets. (**Eric Knox**)

The unfortunate thing for Scotland is that it is not an obviously oppressed nation, as Ireland was, only a visibly depressed one searching for the source of its depression. (**Edwin Muir**)

The Scots are like the English in their underpants. (**William McIlvanney**)

SCOTLAND BY NON-SCOTS

A Scotsman would have asked for separate cheques at the Last Supper. (**Les Dawson**)

Scotland: land of the omnipotent No. (**Alan Bold**)

It is not so much to be lamented that Old England is lost as that the Scottish have found it. (**Samuel Johnson**)

For a marriage to be valid in Scotland, it is absolutely necessary that it should be consummated in the presence of two policemen. (**Samuel Butler**)

The noblest prospect which a Scotsman ever sees is the high road that leads him to England. (**Samuel Johnson**)

God made Scotland but we must remember He also made hell. (**Samuel Johnson**)

What do Scotsmen do when they want to have romantic candle-lit suppers? Scrape the wax out of their girlfriends' ears. (**Bob Monkhouse**)

I have been trying all my life to like Scotchmen but have been obliged to desist from the experiment in despair. (**Charles Lamb**)

Seeing Scotland is like seeing a worse England. It is seeing the flower fade away to the naked stalk. (**Samuel Johnson**)

The three smallest books in the world are the *British Book of Space Achievers*, *Titalian War Heroes*, and the *Scottish Giftbook*. (**Robert McKee**)

In all my travels I never met with a Scotchman that had sense. I believe everybody of that country that has any leaves the country as fast as they can. (**Francis Lockier**)

That garret of the earth, that knuckle-end of England, that land of Calvin, oatcakes and sulphur. (**Sydney Smith**)

Lutherans are like Scottish people only with less frivolity. (**Garrison Keillor**)

A Scotsman was informed that it would require a surgical operation to get a joke into his head. He asked with a puzzled frown, 'And why should I want to get it in?' (***Strand* magazine**)

The reason all the Scots have a sense of humour is because it's free. (**Bob Monkhouse**)

Poor sister Scotland, her doom is fell,
She cannot find any more Stuarts to sell.
(**James Joyce**)

The Scottish are the nymphomaniacs of world rugby. (**George Hook**)

SELF-CRITICISM

I promised I'd take Rotherham out of the First Division. I did – into the Second Division. (**Tommy Docherty**)

It was an easy decision to become a professional darts player. I was unemployed. (**Jocky Wilson**)

I'm a second eleven sort of chap. (**J.M. Barrie**)

I was something of a hellraiser in my youth. If you're out having a good time, all you're fit for the next day is tidying the flat. (**Robbie Coltrane**)

Dad said I had a voice like a coalman. (**Lulu**)

If they'd used video evidence for football matches in my day I'd still be doing time. (**Graeme Souness**)

Most of my lyrics are just bad mother-in-law jokes. (**Billy MacKenzie**)

I'm a devout coward. It's my religion. (**John Dorans**)

I fear I have nothing original inside me except original sin. (**Thomas Campbell**)

It was revealed to me many years ago with conclusive certainty that I was a fool and that I had always been a fool. Since then I have been as happy as any man has a right to be. (**Alastair Sim**)

Whenever I take off my T-shirt to sunbathe I look like a milk bottle. (**Billy Connolly**)

In the days when we were working on The Two Ronnies, our partnership worked well because Ron Barker wrote the material and I queued up for the lunch. (**Ronnie Corbett**)

If I'd been a soldier, the Germans would have won the war. (**Andy Cameron**)

As a journalist I rely on two qualifications: a congenital laziness and a poor memory. (**Wilfred Taylor**)

I have four reasons for not writing: I am too old, too fat, too lazy, and too rich. (**David Hume**)

I was so small and skinny when I was born it's a wonder my father, who was a fisherman, didn't throw me back into the North Sea. (**Denis Law**)

I never regret any mistakes for too long. Mainly because I'm always making new ones. (**Irvine Welsh**)

Kevin Ratcliffe once claimed that my true vocation in life was as a kamikaze pilot. (**Andy Gray**)

Sometimes I feel about as awkward as a left-handed violinist in a crowded string section. (**Chic Murray**)

Whenever I pass a mirror and catch a glimpse of myself I go, 'Nah'. (**Tom Conti**)

My father used to tell me I looked like a tramp peering out of a hayloft. (**Billy Connolly**)

I've had a fair amount of television experience as a soccer commentator, mainly thanks to Scotland's habit of not selecting me for world cups. (**Andy Gray**)

I always miss the golden moments. Take me to any football stadium in the world and it's guaranteed I'll be in the toilet when the winning goal is scored. Get me a free pass to the Playboy mansion and I'll ring the doorbell on the day Hugh Hefner turns the place into a Lutheran retreat. It's the sad, pathetic story of my life. (**Lawrence Donegan**)

I once sat through an entire chat show with my fly undone. It was the most revealing interview I've ever given. (**Sean Connery**)

When I was born my mother looked at me and then looked at the afterbirth and screamed, 'Twins!' (**Derek McGovern**)

I'm a small, balding, Celtic-supporting ex-communist Catholic Unionist. Is it any wonder that everyone seems to hate me? (**John Reid**)

I'm bad at exercising. I once joined a gym but the smell was so appalling I had to be taken outside. (**Bill Nighy**)

SELF-IMAGE

I'm as quiet as a mouse peeing on a blotter. (**Norman McLeod**)

My function during the past twenty to thirty years has been that of the catfish that vitalises the other torpid denizens of the aquarium. (**Hugh McDiarmid**)

I cannot claim that I am not afraid of anything but I am in the next best position: I am not afraid of being afraid. (**R.D. Laing**)

I've often described myself as anally explosive. (**Elaine C. Smith**)

SEX

As long as women say 'I went at sex like a steam engine six times a night' kiss-and-tells are fine. It's when they say you were hung like a hamster and went at it like a tortoise that it can do you untold damage. (**George Graham**)

I never understood the expression 'casual sex'. With me it's always a tempest. (**Billy Connolly**)

Sex is every bit as interesting as agriculture. (**Muriel Spark**)

Don't ever have sex on nylon sheets. It can't be done. Your pubic hair stands on end and sparks fly out of your armpits. (**Billy Connolly**)

A pupil at a Lanarkshire primary school returned home after a sex education lesson so well versed on the subject that he was able to tell his parents 'Boys have got a penis and girls have got a fat China'. (**Tom Shields**)

There's still plenty of lead in the pencil but I only write to one person now. (**Rod Stewart**)

At the divorce hearing she told the judge that during her marriage her man spoke to her only three times. She got the custody of the three weans. (**Stanley Baxter**)

There I was, three sheets to the wind, having a nightcap at the hotel bar when some gorgeous girl came up and started telling me, 'I love your music. I think you're fantastic.' What was I to do, talk to a roadie about guitar strings? (**Midge Ure**)

If Freud had worn a kilt in the prescribed Highland manner, he might have had a different attitude to genitals. (**Anthony Burgess**) OK

Every seven seconds in the world a man has sex. This maniac must be stopped at once. (**Alec Craigie**)

Bill Shankly was against sex before big matches. He used to tell us to wear boxing gloves in bed on Friday nights, and to send the wife back to her mother. (**Ian St. John**)

Jeannie, Jeannie, full of hopes
Read a book by Marie Stopes
But to judge from her condition
She must have read the wrong edition.

(**English nursery rhyme**)

I like being the Thinking Woman's Crumpet. (**Tom Conti**)

If ye want a boy, dae it wi' yer boots on. (**Traditional saying**)

We don't actually have sex in the West of Scotland. We just stand in our underwear and throw chips at each other across the floor. My weans were actually conceived from a bit of bacteria on a mutton pie. (**Ian Pattison**)

Except for the two people who are indulging in it, the sexual act is a comic operation. (**Sir Compton Mackenzie**)

Are there sexy dead ones? (**Sean Connery after being informed he was voted 'The sexiest man alive' in a poll**)

The reason I don't put sex into my books is because it gets in the way of the action. (**Alastair McLean**)

Sex has been so long a vulgar joke that the tendency now is to jump to the opposite extreme and make it unmentionable not because it is too evil, but because it is too good. (**A.S. Neill**)

It's always been a puzzle why baby girls talk earlier than boys. The reason, I can now reveal, is breastfeeding. Boys would rather breastfeed than talk because they know they won't be getting that close again for about fifteen years. (**Derek McGovern**)

SEXISM

My father did the dishes on Christmas Day so my mum could put her feet up. This was his entire contribution to the domestic set-up. (**Rhona Cameron**)

Uncle Harry was an early feminist. My family recounted how, at a race meeting in Ayr, he threw himself under a suffragette. (**Arnold Brown**)

SNOOKER

One of Stephen Hendry's greatest assets is his ability to score when he's playing. (**Ted Lowe**)

You've got to have self-confidence in yourself. (**Stephen Hendry**)

Stephen Hendry jumps on Steve Davis' misses every chance he gets. (**Mike Hallett**)

Seventy-four minutes and 11 seconds. I kid you not: That is the time it took the two dullest players in the history of the game, Peter Ebdon and Graeme Dott, to complete the first frame of the final session in the World Snooker Championship Final. Ronnie O'Sullivan, who was knocked out in the semi-finals, was meanwhile probably touching down in Barbados with a cluster of air hostesses, 147 bottles of pink champagne and every chance of a maximum break. (**Hilary Fannin**)

Hurricane Higgins can either win or lose this final tomorrow. (**Archie McPherson**)

Graeme Dott, the new world snooker champion, is a diehard Rangers fan and he'll be parading the silverware before the Hearts game on Sunday. So at least there will be one trophy at Ibrox this season. (**Tam Cowan in 2006**)

Over the past few years the characters in snooker have disappeared quicker than Jimmy White's bald spot. The highlight of this year's world championship was the tip coming off Ronnie

O' Sullivan's cue. The best laugh you get nowadays is provided by commentator John Virgo. Don't you love it when young players who can hit century breaks with their eyes closed are told what they're doing wrong by the man whose last victory may have been at the Pontin's classic in 1976? (**Tam Cowan**)

I don't smile much and I don't have too big a fan base with blokes, but grannies adore me. (**Stephen Hendry**)

SPEED

The secret of my success over the 400 metres is that I run the first 200 metres as fast as I can. Then, for the second 200 metres, with God's help, I run faster. (**Eric Liddell**)

Dino Zoff is all right with the high balls but with the low ones he goes down in instalments. (**Ian St. John on the former Italian keeper**)

Jackie Stewart was the first of the modern-style drivers, a man who drove fast enough to win but at the lowest possible speed. (**Stirling Moss**)

You're very deceptive, son. You're even slower than you look. (**Tommy Docherty to Leighton James**)

I bowl so slowly that if I don't like a ball I can run after it and bring it back. (**J. M. Barrie**)

Four hours after I began my first book, my son said to me, 'Are you finished it yet, Daddy?' (**A. J. Cronin**)

The Day of Judgment will be at hand when the MacBrayne steamer is on time. (**Ian Crichton-Smith**)

All travelling becomes dull in exact proportion to its rapidity. (**John Ruskin**)

If there's one thing Gus Uhlenbeek's got, it's pace and determination. (**Ray Houghton**)

Graeme Souness was caught speeding last week. He'd do anything for points. (**Gordon Fraser**)

On the Isle of Eigg, asked when the ferry was due, a local replied 'Weel, she'll be coming sometimes sooner and whiles earlier, and sometimes before that again.' (**David Ross**)

Robert Louis Stevenson said it was better to travel hopefully than to arrive. Then again, he never spent an hour in Didcot railway station in the freezing cold of winter. (**Lord Mancroft**)

TACTICS

There was no point in him coming to team talks. All I used to say was, 'Whenever possible, pass the ball to George.' (**Sir Matt Busby on George Best**)

The secret of being a good manager is to keep the six players who hate you away from the five who are undecided. (**Jock Stein**)

Ally MacLeod thinks tactics are a new kind of peppermint. (**Simon Douglas**)

If one day the tacticians reached perfection, the result would be a nil-all draw. And there'd be no one there to see it. (**Paddy Crerand**)

If you played football on a blackboard, Don Howe would win the World Cup every time. (**Willie Johnston**)

WEIGHT

Cricket is the only game where you can actually put on weight when playing. (**Tommy Docherty**)

I've lost a stone and a half in a month with Weight Watchers. I do it on the phone. They run it rather like Alcoholics Anonymous. You get a counsellor and you can call him any time of the day or night if you're being tempted by a packet of chocolate biscuits. (**Robbie Coltrane**)

I cannot but bless the memory of Julius Caesar for the great esteem he expressed for fat men, and his aversion to lean ones. (**David Hume**)

I hate orgies. You have to hold your stomach in for hours on end. (**Billy Connolly**)

There's a thousand nice things happen to you when the weight starts coming off. I got in a plane today and had absolutely no problem getting the lap strap on. (**Robbie Coltrane**)

You can make a player fitter by giving him a pay rise. (**Lou Macari**)

Men look in the mirror, stick out their spare tyres and say things like, 'Aye, there's a lot of beer and money gone into that.' Women see they're a bit overweight and say, 'Oh God I'm fat and ugly, untalented, boring, lazy and unlovable. I think I'll just kill myself.' (**Elaine C. Smith**)

WIVES

No wife can endure a gambling husband ... until he becomes steady winner. (**Lord Thomas Robert Dewar**)

It is with publishers as it is with wives: one always wants somebody else's. (**Norman Douglas**)

One night after dinner and a hard day's work at being a doctor, I vaguely mentioned my longing to do a book. My wife smiled at me kindly over her knitting and led me on to talk about my golf handicap. (**A. J. Cronin**)

People who are dreadfully devoted to their wives are apt, from mere habit, to get devoted to other people's wives as well. (**Jane Welsh Carlyle**)

A loving wife is better than making fifty at cricket. Beyond that I will not go. (**J.M. Barrie**)

The missus is different class. You go in there and say something about the game and all you get back is, 'Ma washing machine is no working, Alex.' (**Alex Ferguson**)

In my day men were content with Ten Commandments and one wife. Now the situation is reversed. (**Saki**)

A Scottish housewife's wages are her food. (**Tommy Leighton**)

I got a dog for the wife. Fair swap, I thought. (**Alex Finlay**)

Lord Byron had two basic maxims: hate your neighbour and love your neighbour's wife. (**Lord Macaulay**)

I canna wive and thrive baith in ae year. (**Allan Ramsay**)

Did you hear about the Scotsman who split his wage packet down the middle every Friday? His wife got the packet and he got the money. (**Bob Monkhouse**)

WOMEN

When a man confront catastrophe on the road he looks in his purse. A woman looks in her mirror. (**Margaret Turnbull**)

Woman wasn't made from man's rib; she was made from his funny bone. (**J. M. Barrie**)

All crises in women's lives seem to be punctuated by cups of tea. (**Willa Muir**)

There is nothing that so thoroughly enthuses the feminine mind as an imaginary injustice perpetrated upon someone unknown to her and under circumstances of which she knows nothing. (**Ian Hay**)

He writes so scathingly of women that, when he treats them in complimentary vein, doubts have been cast upon his authorship. (**J.W. Baxter on William Dunbar**)

Women do not find it difficult nowadays to behave like men but they often find it extremely difficult to behave like gentlemen. (**Compton Mackenzie**)

A woman's grief is like a summer storm – short and violent. (**Joanna Baillie**)

A woman who leaves her cook never wholly recovers her position in society. (**Saki**)

Women have to love before they have sex; men have to have sex before they can love. (**Rhona Henderson**)

A woman is a question which, no matter how you answer it, you must get wrong. (**William McIlvanney**)

WRITERS ON WRITERS

A miserable creature hungering after sweets he can't get. (**Thomas Carlyle on John Keats**)

He might let you tug the hem of his garment once in a while but that was all. (**John Bellamy on Hugh McDiarmid**)

Samuel Pepys was a man known to his contemporaries as a halo of almost historical pomp, and to his remote descendants like a tap-room companion. (**Robert Louis Stevenson**)

Hugh McDiarmid is a symbol of all that's perfectly hideous about Scotland. (**Irvine Welsh**)

Carlyle was so poisonous, it's a wonder his mind didn't infect his bloodstream. (**John Carey**)

I do not know if Bacon wrote the words of Shakespeare or not but if he didn't it seems to me he missed the opportunity of his life. (**J.M. Barrie**)

More nonsense has been uttered in Robbie Burns' name than in anyone barring Jesus Christ. (**Hugh McDiarmid**)

A shaggy, unchained dog scouring the beaches of the world and baying at the moon. (**Robert Louis Stevenson on Walt Whitman**)

I think of Robert Louis Stevenson as a consumptive youth weaving garlands of sad flowers with pale, weak hands. (**George Moore**)

Thomas Carlyle, that arrogant old muddle-head and grumbler, spent his long life trying to romanticise the common sense of his Englishmen – in vain. (**Friedrich Nietzsche**)

Talking to J.B.S. Haldane was like sitting on a landmine about to blow up. (**John Maynard Smith**)

J. M. Barrie was a triumph of sugar over diabetes. (**George Jean Nathan**)

Sir Walter Scott, when all is said and done, is an inspired butler. (**William Hazlitt**)

Bernard Shaw once began an article on a play of mine with the words, 'It's even worse than Shakespeare'. I admit that this rankled. (**J.M. Barrie**)

Lightning Source UK Ltd.
Milton Keynes UK
UKHW02f1001131217
314388UK00006B/87/P